Genetically Modified Food

ISSUES
(formerly Issues for the Nineties)

Volume 47

Editor

Craig Donnellan

Independence
Educational Publishers
Cambridge

First published by Independence
PO Box 295
Cambridge CB1 3XP
England

© Craig Donnellan 2000

Copyright
This book is sold subject to the condition that it shall not,
by way of trade or otherwise, be lent, resold, hired out or otherwise
circulated in any form of binding or cover other than that in which it
is published without the publisher's prior consent.

Photocopy licence
The material in this book is protected by copyright. However, the
purchaser is free to make multiple copies of particular articles for instructional
purposes for immediate use within the purchasing institution.
Making copies of the entire book is not permitted.

British Library Cataloguing in Publication Data
Genetically Modified Food – (Issues Series)
I. Donnellan, Craig II. Series
363.1'92

ISBN 1 86168 118 6

Printed in Great Britain
The Burlington Press
Cambridge

Typeset by
Claire Boyd

Cover
The illustration on the front cover is by
Pumpkin House.

CONTENTS

Chapter One: An Overview

Chapter Two: The GM Debate

Introduction

Genetically Modified Food is the forty-seventh volume in the **Issues** series. The aim of this series is to offer up-to-date information about important issues in our world.

Genetically Modified Food looks at the current debate, the concerns and the benefits.

The information comes from a wide variety of sources and includes:
Government reports and statistics
Newspaper reports and features
Magazine articles and surveys
Literature from lobby groups
and charitable organisations.

It is hoped that, as you read about the many aspects of the issues explored in this book, you will critically evaluate the information presented. It is important that you decide whether you are being presented with facts or opinions. Does the writer give a biased or an unbiased report? If an opinion is being expressed, do you agree with the writer?

Genetically Modified Foods offers a useful starting-point for those who need convenient access to information about the many issues involved. However, it is only a starting-point. At the back of the book is a list of organisations which you may want to contact for further information.

*****

Biotechnology basics

Biotechnology questions and answers

All food sources available have evolved through natural selection. Almost every ingredient used in food production originates from a living organism, be it a plant, a micro-organism or an animal. The rich genetic diversity represented by all these sources was first maximised when farmers began to save the seeds from their best crops for later sowing and to use the best animals for breeding. Therefore biotechnology has always been an intimate part of food production.

New methods based on molecular biology, made possible by major discoveries over the past 50 years building on the pioneering work of Darwin and Pasteur, demonstrate that organisms can be genetically modified. Over twenty Nobel Prizes have been awarded for discoveries in the area of biotechnology, many of them in Europe. These new methods offer the prospect of more rapid and precisely targeted changes than can be introduced through traditional breeding and selection for improving the food chain. Although very few food products derived from modern biotechnology are available as yet, they arouse considerable public interest. Given a clear demand by European consumers for accurate information on modern biotechnology, EUFIC, the European Food Information Council, is taking the necessary steps to help provide this information. It is directly relevant to the food products offered to the consumer. Here are answers to the most frequently asked questions about biotechnology applications in the food chain.

Why focus on food biotechnology these days?

Yesterday, food technology aimed at preserving food to keep it as wholesome as possible and free from contamination. Today, food technology seeks convenience, nutritive quality, and environmental protection. The goals have changed: consumers expect food to be varied, sophisticated, in individual portions, and ready to eat. To satisfy those needs all elements of the food chain are involved: research, harvest, preparation, processing, packaging and retail distribution to the consumer. Biotechnology adds to that improved and better-protected food products, and will be able, in the future, to create entirely new products. European consumers wish to be informed on these developments now that such products are coming to the market and regulations for these novel foods are being issued at European and national levels.

What are the differences in food produced with the help of biotechnology?

Most if not all of the plants used in agriculture are vastly different from their ancestors. Since man began practising agriculture he has looked for improvement of plants and animals by breeding. Nature does it by itself: rape seed is a natural hybrid between cauliflower and turnip. Plant breeders use natural variation to select plants with more desirable properties, such as the wild cabbage from which a variety of food plants resulted: cauliflower, broccoli, red cabbage, etc. Genetic modification is the next logical step. Nowadays it is possible to choose a gene from one species and to introduce it into another to obtain derived improvements. By putting together all the elements used in the improvement of agricultural crops throughout the centuries, it becomes clear that this is an evolutionary process rather than a revolution. One step allows the other to follow in a continuously developing process.

New food products appear as a consequence of consumer demand. What exactly does consumer demand mean?

Food habits are influenced by a number of factors such as the ageing of the European population, the

decrease in job security and the reduction in family size. Choice of food has evolved: products are more diverse, branded, packaged, labelled with information; consumer outlets are more widespread and, finally, food technology has improved. All this changes consumers' food habits and therefore demand. Consumers expect nutritional value, pleasure in eating, confidence in their food and low prices. In addition they wish for more information to help make their choices.

How is the consumer going to be informed?

Labelling is required when the new product is different from the conventional product and when it may have specific implications for the health of certain individuals or particular ethical concerns.

Is labelling the only way to inform consumers?

Labelling is extremely important in informing consumers. Simple comprehensive information will help build consumer confidence. Therefore in addition to labelling, objective data and other information should be provided by scientific experts and specialists within the food chain. News media also have a role to play in providing information to the consumer.

Is biotechnology really necessary?

The applications of biotechnology to plant breeding can offset the vulnerability of crop production to damage caused by diseases and pests leading to losses that quite often are grossly underestimated. The world grain stocks are currently at their lowest level in 30 years and far below the safety level of 60 days' world need set by the United Nations and the FAO. The world needs more reliable food production from crops and livestock. To meet that growing demand, more disease-resistant crops with increased yield potential need to be developed, without expensive arable land expansion and further deforestation.

What are the opportunities opened up by food biotechnology?

It is now possible to carry out genetic

modification on all plant species, including all the world's major crops. Biotechnology has the potential to improve the efficiency of agriculture and to allow sustainable food production in the 21st century. Its goal of improving on currently available foods is the same as that of the traditional, long-established techniques of crop breeding, animal husbandry and fermentation. The major difference is the ability to cross the natural barriers that limit traditional cross breeding and selection.

Resistance is common in nature but not always present in those crops where we want it. Biotechnology now provides the tools to use the natural resistance of one plant in another.

Does biotechnology include the technique of cloning plants and animals?

Cloning of plants has been used for decades in many crops, for example all our potato varieties are clones. Cloning, in fact, means making an exact copy of an existing plant. Cloning of animals has been done for research purposes but not for the production of food.

How are biotechnology food products controlled and regulated?

Today, numerous science- and experience-based guidelines are in place for assessing biosafety issues. These include guidelines from the World Health Organisation (WHO), the Food and Agriculture Organisation (FAO), the OECD group of national experts, the UNIDO, the World Bank/International Service for National Agricultural Research, and the European Novel Foods Regulation.

How can the consumer be sure that biotechnology products are safe?

Biotechnology does not lead to inherently less safe foods than those

developed by conventional techniques, but because it is a new technology, specific attention must be, and is, given to biotechnology. Biotechnology foods are among the most extensively tested foods ever sold in the history of mankind.

Have all the risks of gene modification been evaluated?

Genetic modification is a succession of techniques based on scientific knowledge and practices, and includes the time necessary to assess the facts before products can be approved for the market. Investigation has concentrated on the possibility of risks related to the gene construction, its stability, transferability and the protein(s) it produces, as well as the issues of environmental impact and compositional changes of the final product. To assess whether a new food is substantially equivalent to a conventional food, three main factors are taken into account:

- the composition and characteristics of the traditional product
- the characteristics altered to produce the new food product, and how these change its composition
- the characteristics and composition of the new food compared with the conventional food.

How is the safety of biotechnology food products tested?

The food safety assessment method developed by independent bodies such as the OECD, WHO and FAO is based on a comparison of the new food with its traditional counterpart, not only because of biotechnology, but because of its new characteristics. Differences from conventional foods or new characteristics are then the focus of further safety investigations to ensure that only food which is safe for consumption reaches the market.

Does biotechnology lead to different end products?

Not necessarily. Soya oil obtained from herbicide-resistant soya beans is identical to the oil obtained from traditional beans. Soya meal from herbicide-resistant beans will contain small amounts of another protein, but it will not affect the nutritional value nor the safety of the product. On the other hand, rape seed modified to produce an oil with a higher content of polyunsaturated fatty acids will logically result in an oil with a different composition.

Does biotechnology improve the quality of a food product?

Biotechnology has the potential to make ever further improvements to food supplies in Europe: better taste and aroma, improved functionality, reduced use of chemicals and their impact on the environment, and healthier and safer products at lower costs.

How can biotechnology bring nutritional improvement to certain foods?

Examples of some nutrient-modified foods made possible through biotechnology include:

- Maize, soybeans and rape seed improved to reduce the saturated fat content of cooking oils derived from these crops.
- Potatoes and maize improved to contain more starch and less water. Potatoes with increased starch content absorb less oil when frying, resulting in lighter

and healthier potato chips and french fries.
- Tomatoes, squash and potatoes could be grown to contain higher levels of nutrients such as vitamins C and E and beta-carotene.

What are the potential benefits of genetic improvement?

Some of the benefits we and our children can expect in the future are:

- Foods with a higher content of vitamins, minerals or protein or lower in fat – making it easier to choose a healthy diet.
- Improved keepability of fruits and vegetables.
- Crops able to resist diseases from bacteria and viruses and able to defend themselves against attacks by insects.
- Herbicide-tolerant crops – this means lesser amounts of herbicides can be used to destroy destructive weeds without destroying the crops as well.
- Quicker diagnosis of diseases in plants and animals.
- Together these benefits will lead to improved quality foods, at lower prices, available to more people throughout the world.

Does the ingestion of genetically modified organisms have any long-term effect on health?

Mankind has always eaten genes without danger since most foods contain them: a plant contains from 10,000 to 75,000 genes per cell. Eating an apple means eating hundreds of millions of genes. Genes in plants modified by spontaneous or traditional methods are no different to biologically modified genes. Genes themselves are not toxic. What is important is the product the genes code for.

Could allergens be transferred by biotechnology?

The use of modern biotechnology to transfer genes between plant species raises the possibility that substances may be transferred from one crop to another. But if this substance could trigger allergic reactions in some individuals it must be declared on the label. In the case of crops known to cause allergic reactions, special care is taken to ensure that genes coding for allergens are not transferred to other species.

- The above information is an extract from the EUFIC website: www.eufic.org

© European Food Information Council (EUFIC)

The benefits

Food for our future

Plants

Fewer crops lost

Biotechnology could be used to help reduce losses to our food supplies. For example:

Disease and pest resistance

Genetic modification can be used to make food crops resistant to disease and pests. For example, a variety of maize (corn), first grown in North America, is resistant to the corn borer insect which can destroy up to 20% of a crop. This is achieved by altering the genetic make-up of the plant so that it produces a new protein which enables it to resist the insect. Approximately 20% of the 1998 US maize harvest was genetically modified in this way.

Genetic modification research is also being carried out to make sweet potato plants resistant to the 'feathery mottle virus' which often ruins two-thirds of the African sweet potato harvest. Cucumber, lettuce, tomatoes, peppers and other horticultural crops could also be modified to resist the destructive 'cucumber mosaic virus'.

Disease diagnosis

Crop diseases are difficult to spot, especially in their early stages. Diagnostic kits, utilising biotechnology, will help farmers tell whether or not their crops are infected so that they spray only when absolutely necessary.

Weed control

Weeds are a serious threat to our food crops. General purpose (broad spectrum) herbicides, which kill a wide range of growing soya plants, can only be used before the crop emerges from the soil. Once the crop is visible, more selective (narrow spectrum) herbicides – or weedkillers – have to be used to combat weeds without damaging the crop.

A variety of soya has now been modified to produce a protein which enables it to tolerate the general purpose herbicide, glyphosate. Farmers can therefore control weeds amongst the growing soya plants and choose the optimal time at which to spray.

It is claimed that, since less glyphosate is needed to control the weeds compared with selective weedkillers, this technology offers a number of benefits. Using fewer chemicals is considered better for the environment and also saves energy because of the lower use of farm machinery. Additionally, better crop management leads to higher yields and improved crop quality.

Approximately 30% of the 1998 US soya harvest was modified to tolerate glyphosate. Soya from such US crops is already being used in food products on sale in the UK.

Feeding the world

Although we seem to have more food available than ever before, feeding everyone in the world is still a huge challenge:

- By the year 2000 world consumption of wheat, rice, maize, barley, and other crops could be over two billion tonnes a year.
- During the past 50 years world population has doubled and during the next 50 it will double again. By the year 2040 there could be nearly 10,000 million people to feed.

Ultimately, feeding the world requires political solutions, but biotechnology could also help by reducing crop losses and improving and increasing food supplies.

Improved nutritional value

Higher-protein foods

Lack of protein is a major cause of malnutrition in many countries of the world. Biotechnology could be used to produce palatable, high-protein crops.

For example:

- Transferring genetic traits from pea plants to produce a higher-protein rice.

Modified fat foods

Maize, soya beans, oilseed rape (canola) and other oil crops could be modified to alter their saturated fat content.

A potato with a higher starch content would absorb less oil during frying, providing an alternative method of producing lower-fat products such as chips and crisps.

Higher-vitamin fruit and veg

Some fruits and vegetables could be adapted to contain higher levels of nutrients, for example, vitamins C and E.

Current research suggests these changes could offer some protection against chronic diseases such as certain cancers and heart disease.

Longer-lasting fruit and veg

Genetic modification to slow down softening will provide fruits that last longer. Flavr Savr® tomatoes with this characteristic are sold in the USA. A similar tomato grown in California and processed into tomato purée is on sale in the UK. Slow softening apples, raspberries and melons have also been produced and this benefit is likely to be transferable to other fruit and vegetable crops including bananas, pineapples, sweet peppers, peaches, nectarines, mangoes and strawberries.

How is it done?

- The Flavr Savr® tomato is the first genetically modified whole food on the market in the USA. Tomatoes and soft fruits are usually picked while still under-ripe so that they remain firm during transportation. The modified tomatoes have had their softening gene 'switched off'. This means they can ripen on the vine until they have their full flavour and colour and still remain firm after harvesting. This should provide greater flexibility during transport and handling and give more choice to the consumer.

A copy is made of the gene responsible for the softening enzyme . . . and turned round so that it blocks the message that switches on the softening process . . . resulting in slower softening tomatoes . . . and so less waste.

Drought resistance

Drought resistance in plants would enable farmers to extend both the growing season and number of places where crops could grow. This is not just a problem in hotter countries. Water availability is a limiting factor nearly everywhere plants are grown, even in the UK.

Nitrogen fixing

Plants need nitrogen to grow. Certain bacteria found in the roots of peas

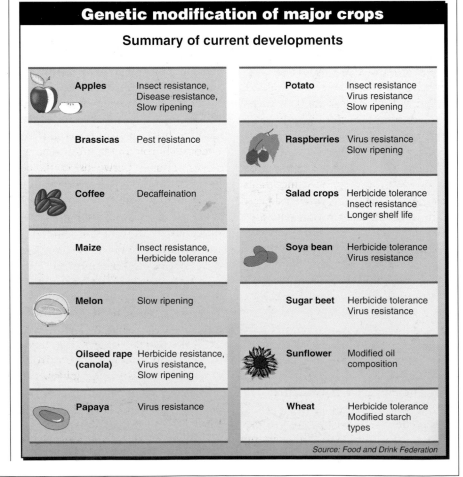

Genetic modification of major crops

Summary of current developments

Crop	Developments	Crop	Developments
Apples	Insect resistance, Disease resistance, Slow ripening	Potato	Insect resistance, Virus resistance, Slow ripening
Brassicas	Pest resistance	Raspberries	Virus resistance, Slow ripening
Coffee	Decaffeination	Salad crops	Herbicide tolerance, Insect resistance, Longer shelf life
Maize	Insect resistance, Herbicide tolerance	Soya bean	Herbicide tolerance, Virus resistance
Melon	Slow ripening	Sugar beet	Herbicide tolerance, Virus resistance
Oilseed rape (canola)	Herbicide resistance, Virus resistance, Slow ripening	Sunflower	Modified oil composition
Papaya	Virus resistance	Wheat	Herbicide tolerance, Modified starch types

Source: Food and Drink Federation

and beans can take nitrogen from the air and convert, or 'fix', it for use in plant growth. Scientists are trying to use genetic modification so that these bacteria can live in the roots of cereal crops to provide a ready-made source of fertiliser. This could be cheaper and more environmentally friendly than the fertilisers we use today.

Frost damage

Frost damage can ruin many crops. Work is under-way to produce plants with an inbuilt mechanism to help fight frost damage. One possibility would involve utilising the gene in fish which enables them to tolerate extreme cold. However, the prospect of copying and transferring 'animal' genes to plants is controversial. It remains to be seen whether or not this would be acceptable to the public.

• The above information is an extract from the Food and Drink Federation web site which can be found at www.foodfuture.org.uk

Also see their address details on page 41.

© *Food and Drink Federation*

The concerns

Food for the future

Is it safe?

Opponents of genetic modification argue that we do not know enough about the science and that altering genes could lead to unforeseen problems for future generations.

Against that it is argued that strict controls are in place and each modified product is very thoroughly assessed for any difference from its conventional counterpart. In addition, since only the specific genes for a trait are identified and copied, the technology is far more precise than the trial-and-error approach of traditional plant and animal breeding.

What laws exist?

In the UK, the Food Safety Act requires that ALL food must be fit for consumption, i.e. must not be injurious to health, be unfit or contaminated.

A specific set of safeguards controls the use of genetic modification in foods or food ingredients. These foods are assessed by a number of committees of independent experts, most of which include consumer representatives:

- The Advisory Committee on Novel Foods and Processes (ACNFP)
- The Committee on Toxicity of Chemicals in Food, Consumer Products and the Environment (COT)
- The Food Advisory Committee (FAC)

The Annual Reports of these Committees are a useful starting point for those who wish to check if,

and how, issues of concern are being addressed.

At European level, the Regulation on Novel Foods and Novel Food Ingredients has been adopted, after four and a half years of discussion. It came into force on 15 May 1997 to harmonise procedures for the approval of all novel foods, including those produced using modern biotechnology. This legislation formalises the UK's previous voluntary procedures which provided a blueprint for the European scheme.

What about the environment?

A main concern is that copy genes incorporated into a plant could 'escape' and transfer to another species with unwanted consequences. For example, it is argued that herbicide-tolerant crops could cross-pollinate with weeds and so become herbicide-tolerant themselves. Thus 'superweeds' could be created.

Some consumers and farmers are also concerned that making crops herbicide-tolerant might lead to an increase in herbicide use, as the crops could withstand higher doses.

Supporters of biotechnology argue that stringent rules exist to safeguard against these possibilities and that the development of genetically modified plants will mean a decrease in the use of environmentally unfriendly herbicides.

What laws exist?

UK regulations (in addition to the EU Novel Foods Regulation) which implement European Directives,

control laboratory experiments, field trials and commercial use are:
- The Genetically Modified Organisms (Contained Use) Regulations 1992
- The Genetically Modified Organisms (Deliberate Release) Regulations 1992

The UK regulatory bodies are the Health and Safety Executive and the Department of the Environment, Transport and the Regions. The latter is advised by the Advisory Committee for Releases to the Environment (ACRE) which is responsible for assessing all applications for releasing genetically modified organisms into the environment in the UK.

Extensive risk-assessment trials are also being carried out in various countries to assess the environmental impact of releasing genetically modified plants. Again, the Annual Reports of these bodies are a useful starting point for those who wish to check if, and how, issues of concern are being addressed. As with the subject of safety, it will remain important that consumer groups continue to be informed and to play a part in the decision-making process.

What about labelling?

Special rules govern the labelling of all foods regarded as 'novel'; these include genetically modified foods. According to the EU Regulation on Novel Foods and Novel Food Ingredients, adopted in 1997, such foods must be labelled if they are 'no longer equivalent' to their conventional counterparts. This would include when they have a different composition, use or nutritional value to the conventional food. Thus for example, fruit and vegetables genetically modified to be higher in certain vitamins would be covered by this Regulation.

Ethical concerns are also covered. For example, since vegetarians might object to incorporating copy genes from animals into plants, such a plant would have to be labelled.

Soya and maize

The first varieties of genetically modified soya and maize were approved, prior to the adoption of the Novel Foods Regulation, under the EU legislation which dealt with the release of genetically modified organisms. This approval did not impose specific labelling requirements. However, in response to consumer pressure, the EU decided that these soya and maize crops should be made subject to the Novel Foods Regulation. They therefore had to consider how the labelling obligations would apply to products made from such crops.

Their decision resulted in a further EU regulation. This stated that foods which contain any genetically modified protein or DNA from the soya and maize crops must be labelled, subject to certain exemptions. In other words the EU has decided that the presence of just a fragment of genetically modified protein or DNA is enough to make the product 'no longer equivalent' to conventional products. The same rules are likely to be applied to other genetically modified foods and ingredients as they are introduced.

The new regulation specifically exempts food additives and flavourings from labelling. It also provides for a 'negative list' of products to be drawn up. This will identify those products derived from soya and maize where it is known that genetically modified protein or DNA is not present. Examples are soya oil, maize oil and glucose (derived from maize starch).

Practical considerations

The new labelling regulation has broadened the scope of labelling required for genetically modified foods, but there are still some practical aspects being considered. In particular, threshold levels have yet to be agreed. These recognise that many foods and food ingredients are produced and sold on a very large scale. At different stages in the food chain, some unintentional 'co-mingling' of products derived from genetically modified crops with those from non-genetically modified crops is bound to happen. Exempting foods from labelling where only a tiny amount of the genetically modified material may be present is considered by most to be a pragmatic approach.

Update May 1999: In implementing the EU labelling Regulation in March 1999, the UK Government has extended the labelling requirement to products sold in restaurants and other catering establishments.

Some consumers would like to have genetically modified crops kept separate from conventional crops so that they can choose to purchase foods 'free from' genetically modified ingredients. Such general segregation would cause considerable practical problems as the unmodified crops and their derivatives would have to be handled separately at every stage of the supply chain. This would inevitably add to their cost and so it remains to be seen if such markets will be viable in the long term.

Another practical consideration arises when genetically modified foods become ingredients in other foods. For example, a corn oil genetically modified to be lower in saturated fat would clearly have to be labelled as produced from genetically modified maize. But if that oil was incorporated into a spread which was then used on sandwiches, would those sandwiches have to be similarly labelled? As with all aspects of labelling law, the point at which the line should be drawn is likely to be the subject of continuing debate.

Meanwhile, consumers can find out more about genetically modified foods via customer care telephone lines and the many consumer leaflets provided by the industry and retailers.

Who should own the rights?

Patent laws protect inventions for a fixed number of years. During this period no one else can copy or use the invention without permission, which usually has to be paid for. Should patent protection extend to genetic modification of foods?

The case for:
- Patent protection enables inventors to recoup their considerable investments in research and development; without it, far less research funding would be available.
- A prerequisite of patent protection is that the details of the patent must be published. Without patent protection, more inventions would be kept secret, which would slow up the development of the science.

The case against:
- Genes are not 'inventions' and therefore should not be subject to patent rights. Life should not be patentable.
- It is wrong that our food supplies could be controlled by the few who can afford the development costs. Food should be available to all.
- Patents tend to benefit the developed countries exclusively; it is important that developing countries have access to these important new technologies.

These conflicting viewpoints have been debated at length at EU level. A new Directive for the legal protection of biotechnological inventions was adopted on 16 June 1998. The Directive grants patent protection for genes and genetically engineered plants and animals provided an invention has been made. The mere discovery of the function of a specific gene cannot be patented. In the case of patents on animals, a 'morality clause' requires patent examiners to weigh up the level of suffering to the animal against the benefit to human or veterinary medicine.

Will developing countries benefit?

The case for:
- Crops could be especially adapted to the diverse farming conditions and practices, and offer greater nutritional value and a higher income.

- Energy-producing crops could also save natural resources and so conserve the environment.

The case against:
- Genetically modified products could reduce the developed countries' reliance on crops from developing countries. This could result in loss of trade and severe economic damage.
- Others doubt whether developing countries will actually receive the benefits.

These issues raise important political, ethical and trade questions which are not unique to modern biotechnology. They must be resolved at government and inter-governmental level to make sure that everyone benefits from the new technology.

What about the gene pool?

Another concern is that wide use of the technology would reduce the diversity of crop species grown and so reduce the 'gene pool'. The gene pool has already been reduced to some extent by modern farming techniques and it is feared that the availability of genetically modified crops would exacerbate the problem. One partial solution lies in storing samples of all plant species in 'gene banks'. Such establishments have already been set up.

Is it ethical?

Most people find the idea of genetically modifying plants acceptable, although some people disagree with all genetic modification on the grounds that we should not tamper with nature.

There is also concern about the possibility of transferring genes of animal or human origin to other animal species and plants.

However, the current consensus among scientists is that whilst the use of human copy genes in food production is theoretically possible, in practice it is very unlikely to be pursued. The use of animal copy genes in plants is more likely, but still very much dependent on consumer acceptance.

The Polkinghorne Committee

In 1993, the UK Government set up a committee to consider these points, chaired by the Reverend Dr Sir John Polkinghorne. It found that:
- Most Christian and Jewish groups in general find genetic modification acceptable;
- Muslims, Sikhs and Hindus have ethical objections to consuming organisms containing copy genes from animals which are the subject of dietary restrictions for their religion;
- Strict vegetarians would object to incorporating copy genes of animal origin in a plant.

The Committee recommended that, should either of the latter two events happen, clear labelling would be required to allow those groups to make an informed choice. This is now a requirement of the EU Novel Foods Regulation.

What about animal welfare?

Related to ethical issues are questions of animal welfare. Consumers are concerned that increasing yields from animals or adapting them to tolerate different environments could lead to distress for the animal. The controversy surrounding the potential for increasing milk yields by using the growth hormone Bovine somatotropin (BST) illustrates the level of consumers' concerns.

In addition, animal welfare supporters stress that mankind has a moral obligation to care for animals and to respect their intrinsic value. It is therefore essential that all animal production, whether or not it involves modern biotechnology, clearly meets recognised standards of animal welfare.

Conclusion

Some of the concerns outlined in this information can be resolved by making more facts available to consumers. Others are more a matter of opinion and need to be discussed further.

The biotechnology debate, involving governments, scientists, industry and consumer groups, is well under way. However, further wide-ranging and open discussions must take place so that all concerns can be properly addressed. Only then can we all benefit from the potential of the new technology.

• The above information is an extract from the Food and Drink Federation web site which can be found on www.foodfuture.org.uk

Also see their address details on page 41.

© *Food and Drink Federation*

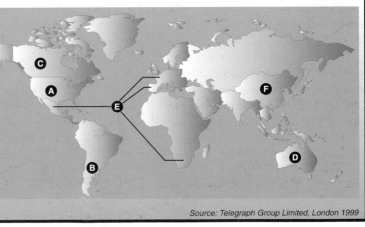

Where GM foods are grown

Countries growing commercial GM crops, with acreage, crops in use and % of market

A The United States: 49.5 million acres, mainly wheat, maize, cotton, canola (74% of world production).

B Argentina: 10.6 million acres, mainly soya (15% of production).

C Canada: 6.9 million acres, mainly maize, canola (10% of production).

D Australia: 240,000 acres (less than 1% of production).

E Mexico, Spain, France and South Africa: have some GM crops, all less than 0.1% of world production.

F China: a rogue state, definitely growing all kinds of GMOs including rice, carp and poplar trees but statistics on what has been released commercially are hard to come by. Most of what goes on there is not available to the world's scientific community and may or may not infringe Western copyrights.

Source: Telegraph Group Limited, London 1999

Questions about genetically modified organisms

An article by The Prince of Wales which appeared in the *Daily Mail*

Summary

The debate about the use of GM technology continues, with daily news of claims about the safety or the risks. The public's reaction shows instinctive nervousness about tampering with nature when we don't know all the consequences. There are unanswered questions which need to be asked – about the need for GM food, its safety, the environmental consequences, consumer choice and the usefulness to feed the world's growing population.

At the end of last year I set up a discussion forum on my website on the question of GMOs. I wanted to encourage wider public debate about what I see as a fundamental issue and one which affects each and every one of us, and future generations.

There was a huge response – some 10,000 replies have indicated that public concern about the use of GM technology has been growing. Many food producers and retailers have clearly felt the same overwhelming anxiety from their consumers who are demanding a choice in what they eat. A number of them have now banned GM ingredients from their own-brand products.

But the debate continues to rage. Not a day goes by without some new piece of research claiming to demonstrate either the safety or the risks of GM technology. It is very hard for people to know just who is right. Few of us are able to interpret all the scientific information which is available – and even the experts don't always agree. But what I believe the public's reaction shows is that instinctively we are nervous about tampering with Nature when we can't be sure that we know enough about all the consequences.

Having followed this debate very closely for some while now, I believe that there are still a number of unanswered questions which need to be asked.

1. Do we need GM food in this country?

On the basis of what we have seen so far, we don't appear to need it at all. The benefits, such as there are, seem to be limited to the people who own the technology and the people who farm on an industrialised scale. We are constantly told that this technology may have huge benefits for the future. Well, perhaps. But we have all heard claims like that before and they don't always come true in the long run – look at the case of antibiotic growth promoters in animal feedstuff . . .

2. Is GM food safe for us to eat?

There is certainly no evidence to the contrary. But how much evidence do we have? And are we looking at the right things? The major decisions about what can be grown and what can be sold are taken on the basis of studying what is known about the original plant, comparing it to the genetically modified variety, and then deciding whether the two are

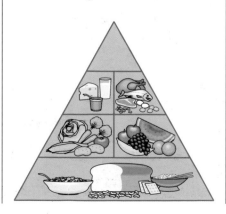

'substantially equivalent'. But is it enough to look only at what is already known? Isn't there at least a possibility that the new crops (particularly those that have been made resistant to antibiotics) will behave in unexpected ways, producing toxic or allergic reactions? Only independent scientific research, over a long period, can provide the final answer.

3. Why are the rules for approving GM foods so much less stringent than those for new medicines produced using the same technology?

Before drugs are released into the marketplace they have to undergo the most rigorous testing – and quite right too. But GM food is also designed in a laboratory for human consumption, albeit in different circumstances. Surely it is equally important that we are confident that it will do us no harm?

4. How much do we really know about the environmental consequences of GM crops?

Laboratory tests showing that pollen from GM maize in the United States caused damage to the caterpillars of Monarch butterflies provide the latest cause for concern. If GM plants can do this to butterflies, what damage might they cause to other species? But more alarmingly perhaps, this GM maize is not under test. It is already .being grown commercially throughout large areas of the United States of America. Surely this effect should have been discovered by the company producing the seeds, or the regulatory authorities who approved them for sale, at a much earlier stage? Indeed, how much more are we going to learn the hard way about the impact of GM crops on the environment?

5. Is it sensible to plant test crops without strict regulations in place?

Such crops are being planted in this country now – under a voluntary code of practice. But English Nature, the Government's official adviser on nature conservation, has argued that we ought to put strict, enforceable regulations in place first. Even then, will it really be possible to prevent contamination of nearby wildlife or crops, whether organic or not? Since bees and the wind don't obey any sort of rules – voluntary or statutory – we shall soon have an unprecedented and unethical situation in which one farmer's crops will contaminate another's against his will.

6. How will consumers be able to exercise genuine choice?

Labelling schemes clearly have a role to play. But if conventional and organic crops can become contaminated by GM crops grown nearby, those people who wish to be sure they are eating or growing absolutely natural, non-industrialised, *real* food, will be denied that choice. This seems to me to be wrong.

7. If something goes wrong with a GM crop, who will be held responsible?

It is important that we know precisely who is going to be legally liable to pay for any damage – whether it be to human health, the environment, or both. Will it be the company who sells the seed or the farmer who grows it? Or will it, as was the case with BSE, be all of us?

8. Are GM crops really the only way to feed the world's growing population?

This argument sounds suspiciously like emotional blackmail to me. Is there any serious academic research to substantiate such a sweeping statement? The countries which might be expected to benefit certainly take a different view. Representatives of 20 African states, including Ethiopia, have published a statement denying that gene technologies will 'help farmers to produce the food that is needed in the 21st Century'. On the contrary, they 'think it will destroy the diversity, the local knowledge and the sustainable agricultural systems … and undermine our capacity to feed ourselves'. How much more could we achieve if all the research funds currently devoted to fashionable GM techniques – which run into billions of dollars a year – were applied to improving methods of agriculture which have stood the test of time? We already know that yields from many traditional farming systems can be doubled, at least, by making better use of existing natural resources.

9. What effect will GM crops have on the people of the world's poorest countries?

Christian Aid has just published a devastating report, entitled *Selling Suicide*, explaining why GM crops are unlikely to provide solutions to the problems of famine and poverty. Where people are starving, lack of food is rarely the underlying cause. It is more likely to be lack of money to buy food, distribution problems or political difficulties. The need is to create sustainable livelihoods for everyone. Will GM crops really do anything to help? Or will they make the problems worse, leading to increasingly industrialised forms of agriculture, with larger farms, crops grown for export while indigenous populations starve, and more displaced farm workers heading for a miserable, degraded existence in yet more shanty towns?

10. What sort of world do we want to live in?

This is the biggest question of all. I raise it because the capacity of GM technology to change our world has brought us to a crossroads of fundamental importance. Are we going to allow the industrialisation of Life itself, redesigning the natural world for the sake of convenience and embarking on an Orwellian future? And, if we do, will there eventually be a price to pay? Or should we be adopting a gentler, more considered approach, seeking always to work with the grain of Nature in making better, more sustainable use of what we have, for the long-term benefit of mankind as a whole? The answer is important. It will affect far more than the food we eat; it will determine the sort of world we, and our children, inhabit.

• The above information is an extract from the Prince of Wales' web site : www.princeofwales.gov.uk

Ten comments from a puzzled subject

Prince Charles created a furore earlier this year by raising ten questions about genetically modified food. *Feedback* asked biotechnology expert Professor Derek Burke to answer them. This is what he came up with

It is not often that a member of the Royal Family, and the heir to the throne to boot, deliberately takes sides in a current debate – and a debate that requires a wide technical knowledge as well as an understanding of current public attitudes. But since he has got involved, I take it that anyone else can get involved too?

1. Do we need GM food in this country?

Not now you may say; we have enough. But food has become cheaper, and better throughout my life – I grew up in a family where chicken was an annual treat – because farmers have used every new technology to our benefit. We can do the same with GM and use the higher yields to stop using marginal land and to restore the hills and coastal strips to their natural state. And when have we British turned our backs on a new technology? New technologies are not all good or all bad: they change things and they pose new questions. So why should we run away from GM?

2. Is GM food safe for us to eat?

Just what is the basis for treating GM foods as so intrinsically dangerous that they should be regarded as the Devil's concoction? Why so black and white? Of course it would be possible to make GM 'food' that was dangerous, but I contend that the three GM foods approved for sale in the UK – cheese, tomato paste and soya – are as safe to eat as any other, and I have no hesitation in doing so. Why not treat food on its merits?

3. Why are the rules for approving GM foods so much less stringent than those for new medicines produced using the same technology?

This is a 'when did you stop beating your wife?' question. The answer has

already been given in the question. The answer is clear: the rules are less stringent, they are different and the same as used elsewhere in the world. Drugs are tested on animals at hundreds of times their clinical doses; that is not possible with food, so different ways have been devised. But if you really want to start trials in humans, 300 million Americans have been eating GM soya for several years now without any ill effects.

4. How much do we really know about the environmental consequences of GM crops?

A huge area – one and a half times the size of Britain – is now sown with GM in North America and, although the environment is not the same, there have been no big problems. The well-publicised experiments with the Monarch butterfly show that under laboratory conditions caterpillars force-fed corn pollen are damaged, but it is unlikely that in the wild the caterpillars would eat corn pollen at all. The effect is small and needs to be guarded against but it is not the catastrophe that some claim.

5. Is it sensible to plant test crops without strict regulations in place?

We already have EU regulations which have the force of law. Now we are using a voluntary code of practice that goes beyond EU rules, is voluntary because we don't want to wait for the EU, and which is overseen by an independent body recently appointed by the minister.

We need these trials so that real choices can be made about appropriate regulation, and so it is important that vandals do not destroy them and that farmers are not put under pressure by green groups to abandon them.

6. How will consumers be able to exercise genuine choice?

Consumers had choice over the first two products, and only when GM soya was introduced was choice lost. Now the emotional campaign against GM foods has removed choice for those of us who want to eat GM soya. So who is being autocratic now? I notice too that the Prince has removed choice from those farmers who farm on his land. Why don't the farmers have choice like US farmers do? There is absolutely no evidence of risk.

7. If something goes wrong with a GM crop who would be held responsible?

Exactly the same bodies as before; for we have been introducing new crops for years – oilseed rape and short-stalked wheat, for example – and there have always been mechanisms for dealing with any damage. To pretend otherwise is misleading.

8. Are GM crops really the only way to feed the world's growing population?

No one has ever said it was, but it seems perverse, even criminal, to walk away from an increased source of food when we need it desperately. And it can help; a new rice with increased vitamin A and iron content is almost ready to meet a huge need in South-East Asia for a population where blindness and anaemia are serious problems.

9. What effect will GM crops have on people of the world's poorest countries?

The Nuffield Council on Bioethics in its recent report points out that, with care, this new technology can help the poorest; a challenge that it is unwise, I suggest even immoral, to walk away from.

10. What sort of world do we want to live in?

I do not want either of the Prince's worlds; neither the Orwellian future nor his organic world, and fortunately for nearly everyone there are many other choices. I want a world where we use technology safely and constructively and we can do that if we keep our heads, which at the moment we are signally failing to do.

• Professor Burke's career was spent in university research and teaching, helping to start a biotechnology company in North America, as a University Vice-Chancellor and for nine years Chairman of the Advisory Committee on Novel Foods and Processes, the regulatory body for all novel foods for human consumption in the UK. He was a member of the Nuffield Council on Bioethics working party which has just produced its Report *Genetically Modified Crops: the ethical and social issues.*
• First published in *Feedback* produced by the Food and Drink Federation

© Food and Drink Federation

GM foods

Questions and answers

The *Guardian* yesterday asked the government to answer Prince Charles' 10 fears for GM food

1. Do we need GM food in this country?

The Prince: The benefits, such as there are, seem to be limited to the people who own the technology and the people who farm on an industrialised scale.

The Government: Biotechnology offers enormous opportunities for improving the quality of life in terms of health, agriculture, food and environmental protection.

2. Is GM food safe for us to eat?

The Prince: Only independent scientific research, over a long period, can provide the final answer.

The Government: That is a question for the scientists not politicians. The Government's top priorities are protecting human health and the environment.

3. Why are the final rules for approving GM foods so much less stringent than those for new medicines produced using the same technology?

The Prince: Before drugs are released on to the market they have to undergo the most rigorous testing…Surely it is equally important that [GM foods] will do us no harm.

The Government: Before crops are approved for planting they are subject to several years of testing for adverse effects.

4. How much do we really know about the environmental consequences of GM crops?

The Prince: Lab tests showing that pollen from GM maize in the United States caused damage to the caterpillars of Monarch butterflies provide the latest cause for concern. More alarmingly, this GM maize is not under test.

The Government: Says it recognises the concerns of people who feel that there may be unforeseen long-term effects on the environment. That is why large-scale independent monitoring and testing is so important.

5. Is it sensible to plant test crops without strict regulations in place?

The Prince: Such crops are being planted in this country now – under a voluntary code of practice. But English Nature has argued that enforceable regulations should be in place first.

The Government: New safeguards and a system of enforcement have been agreed between the industry and the Government which could form basis of future statutory or regulatory intervention.

6. How will consumers be able to exercise genuine choice?

The Prince: Labelling schemes clearly have a role to play, but if conventional and organic crops are contaminated by GM crops, people who wish to avoid GM food products will be denied choice.

The Government: This Government was the first to introduce labelling for GM foods. The testing process will establish the dangers, if any, of contamination of non-GM crops.

7. If something goes wrong with a GM crop, who will be held responsible?

The Prince: It is important that we know precisely who is going to be legally liable to pay for any damage

– whether it be to human health, the environment or both.

The Government: The issue of liability is being discussed but no regulations have been put in place. If a commercial GM crop is shown to have adverse effects, the Government will have the power to have it removed.

8. Are GM crops really the only way to feed the world's growing population?

The Prince: This arguments sounds suspiciously like emotional blackmail to me.

The Government: That is a question for the scientists. Government emphasises the enormous benefits from GM crops such as pest resistance.

9. What effect will GM crops have on the people of the world's poorest countries?

The Prince: Where people are starving, lack of food is rarely the underlying cause. The need is to create sustainable livelihoods for everyone. Will GM crops really help

or will they make the problems worse?

The Government: Say they are taking steps to ensure that individual states have power over ability of multinationals to move GM crops and foods between countries.

10. What sort of world do we want to live in?

The Prince: Are we going to allow the industrialisation of Life itself, redesigning the natural world for the sake of convenience? Or should we be adopting a gentler, more considered approach, seeking always to work with the grain of nature?

The Government: A safe one. That is why we are proceeding extremely cautiously.

© The Guardian,
June, 1999

Genetically modified food

Information from the Society, Religion and Technology Project, Church of Scotland

Some see genetic engineering opening up great opportunities in agriculture, food and medicine as we learn to harness the power of the gene.

For others it's a threat to something very basic about ourselves and the natural world, unnecessary, harmful, unethical, and mostly benefiting big business at others' expense.

Should we be doing genetic modification?

Some Christians object in principle to genetically modified food, as an unacceptable intervention in God's creation. Others see the potential for using God's gift of our technical skills, but with strong provisos, on matters of food safety and environmental risk. Christians believe that humans and all of God's creatures are much more than their genes. To change one or two genes would not make an organism less than itself, but the change would be unacceptable for some, even so.

Should we be eating animal genes or even human genes?

Many people ask if it would be cannibalism to eat food that contained a gene of human origin, or ceremonially unclean for a Jew or Muslim, say, to eat food with a pig gene. At the moment such products are not envisaged, out of respect for these very questions. Before a gene is transferred from one organism to another it is copied millions of times, so the chances of eating the same gene are tiny, but a pig gene doesn't cease to be pig by copying it. What matters to most is where it originally came from, and the genetic information, which of course is still the same.

Who benefits, who loses?

Food is a special case. It is so basic to us all that anyone proposing to make substantial changes to what we are offered to eat must take the greatest care to listen to the public and respect their views beforehand. Those who have objections to genetically

modified food should not be put at a disadvantage, whether or not most people share their concerns. It is a matter of justice that people should not have to pay more for what up till now has been 'normal' food. There should be a legal requirement to label all foodstuffs which contain significant amounts of genetically modified constituents, and steps should be taken to ensure the proper segregation of source materials. At the moment the UK legislation is lax on both these points, and some are disadvantaged as a result.

Problems with genetically engineered soya bean and maize imports

It is one thing to have a single genetically modified product like a tomato, which is clearly labelled. Soya and maize, however, are staple commodities in food processing. In December 1996 the EU accepted the import of genetically modified soya bean and maize. They will go untraced into a large number of foodstuffs. Ordinary people have had little say in these decisions, and there is a sense of imposition without due public discussion. The impression is of more concern with winning markets than public attitudes. Just when the general public is uncertain whether it wants this new technology or not, it seems foolish to put on to the market genetically modified versions of the very foods which are so widely used in processing that almost any food will contain them.

The risk is that, as with irradiated food, the public might vote with its feet about genetically modified food.

Will genetic engineering really feed the world?

Claims are often made for the potential of genetically modified food to 'feed the world'. For example, if genes could be manipulated to enable staple crops to grow in what are today marginal conditions, it could make a big difference to many countries which struggle to feed themselves. However Christians are concerned that the driving forces of biotechnology are leading us to create unnecessary products for western indulgence, when the real food shortages elsewhere in the world remain neglected. Technically these areas are proving difficult, and financially there is less return than products for our supermarkets. But the claim to feed the world will not be taken seriously, if so little biotechnological investment and expertise is focused on the needs of marginal agriculture in the Third World. Sooner or later there have to be some tangible results, if genetic engineering is not just to be another 'rich man's' technology.

Genetically modified food – the objections

- Should we be modifying genes at all?
- It's 'playing God' or unnatural.
- It's wrong to mix genes from radically different organisms.
- Religious and vegetarian groups would object to genes from some species.

- Do we really know what we're doing?
- Have we evaluated the risks sufficiently?
- Is it really necessary?
- Do we need genetically modified food?
- It is just going to provide luxuries for the rich, and won't feed the Third World.
- Agriculture is already too technological. This will only make it worse.
- There better ways to improve resistance and reduce chemicals on the land.
- Do we have a real say in what's going on?
- Labelling measures are inadequate, and unjust towards those who object.
- Big business is imposing on our freedom under the guise of free trade.
- Government committees do not represent ordinary people enough.
- Do supermarkets act as enough of a voice for you and me?
- Religious and vegetarian groups will be put at a disadvantage.

Genetically modified food – the case in favour

- We shouldn't be afraid of biotechnology
- Why draw the line here, not elsewhere?
- We have many safeguards in place.
- Changing one or two genes does not make a foodstuff unacceptable.

- We are more than just our genes.
- Look at the opportunities for good.
- Better resistance to weeds, pests, disease.
- Better texture, flavour, nutritional value.
- Longer shelf life, easier shipment.
- Better yield, more efficient use of land.
- Less herbicides and other chemicals.
- Essential if we are to feed the world.
- The economic and employment case.
- Opportunities for Scottish innovation to benefit the people of Scotland.
- If we pull out, jobs and wealth we might have created will go abroad instead.

The democratic case

- With labelling, adequate protection can be given for those who object.
- Several ethics and safety advisory committees represent public concerns.
- If you don't like it, write to your MP!
- The market is the best ethical judge: if people don't want it they won't buy it.

• The above information is from the Society, Religion and Technology Project of the Church of Scotland. See page 41 for address details.

© Donald M. Bruce, 1999

Biotech primer

Information from Monsanto's web site

What has come to be called 'biotechnology' and the genetic manipulation of agricultural products is nothing new. Indeed, it may be one of the oldest human activities. For thousands of years, from the time human communities began to settle in one place, cultivate crops and farm the land, humans have manipulated the genetic nature of the crops and animals they raise. Crops have been bred to improve yields, enhance taste and extend the growing season. Each of the 15 major crop plants, which provide 90 per cent of the globe's food and energy intake, has been extensively manipulated, hybridised, inter-bred and modified over the millennia by countless generations of farmers intent on producing crops in the most effective and efficient ways possible.

Today, biotechnology holds out promise for consumers seeking quality, safety and taste in their food choices; for farmers seeking new methods to improve their productivity and profitability; and for governments and non-governmental public advocates seeking to stave off global hunger, assure environmental quality, preserve biodiversity and promote health and food safety.

We at Monsanto invite you to learn more about the basics of food biotechnology by exploring the information below.

Frequently asked questions

Why do we need this technology?

Demand for food is increasing dramatically as the world's population grows. Biotechnology provides us with a way of meeting this growing demand without placing even greater pressure on our scarce resources. It allows us to grow better quality crops with higher yields while at the same time sustaining and protecting the environment. It can also help to improve the nutritional value of the crops which are grown.

What is genetic modification?

Genetic modification is an accurate and effective way of achieving more desirable characteristics in plants without the trial and error of traditional methods of selective breeding.

For centuries farmers and gardeners have attempted to alter and improve the plants they grow. In the past this was done by cross-breeding one plant or flower with another in the hope of producing a plant with particular qualities such as a larger flower or a sweeter fruit. The processes used in the past attempted to bring about changes in plants by combining all the characteristics of one plant with those of another.

But as our understanding of plant life has grown, scientists have found ways of speeding up this process and making it more precise and reliable. It is now possible to identify exactly which genes are responsible for which traits. Using this information, scientists can make small and specific changes to a plant without affecting it in other ways.

An example of this is a potato which has been genetically modified to give it a built-in resistance to the Colorado beetle which can destroy potato crops thus reducing the need for chemical pesticides.

What sort of changes can be brought about by genetic modification?

Plants can be modified to bring about many changes which can be of benefit to consumers, the food industry, farmers and people in the developing world. Genetic modification can also contribute towards a more sustainable form of agriculture and bring environmental benefits.

- Fruit and vegetables can be modified to improve their taste and appearance. This means being able to provide consumers with the consistently high quality fresh produce they demand.
- Improvements can be made to the nutritional qualities of certain plants. For example oil seed, from which some cooking oils are made, can be developed so that the oil has a reduced saturated fat content.
- Products can be modified in ways which will make it easier and cheaper to process them. For example the modification of tomatoes to delay ripening has led to cheaper tomato purée.
- Plants can be modified to increase their ability to fight insects, disease and weeds, all of which can destroy or seriously damage crops. This not only increases the yield of these crops, but also reduces the need for pesticides.
- Plants can be modified to be resistant to drought or to grow in difficult conditions. This will have many benefits for parts of the world where the demand for food is increasing significantly and there is not enough good arable land.

How can we assure that these new developments are safe?

It is important that consumers feel confident about the food they buy. Modern biotechnology is therefore subject to strict controls. These are designed to ensure that new genetically modified products are safe to eat and that they pose no new risks to the environment.

European legislation on novel foods is implemented in the UK by a strict regulatory process involving a number of different committees, each composed of independent experts. Many of these people are scientists but the committees also include individuals who are primarily concerned with ethical and consumer issues.

How do we know that genetically modified crops are safe to eat?

Before any genetically modified food can be sold or grown, it has to go through a rigorous approval process.

The main committees responsible for food safety are:

- The Advisory Committee on Novel Foods and Processes (ACNFP)
- The Committee on Toxicity of Chemicals in Foods, Consumer Products and the Environment (COT)
- The Food Advisory Committee (FAC)

In order to ensure openness and accountability, the proceedings of these committees are available to the public.

Some people who question genetic modification argue that we do not know enough about the long-term impact of what is being done and that altering genes could lead to unforeseen problems in the future. There is, however, in spite of widespread research, still no evidence to support this view. In order to continue to protect the interests of consumers, the Advisory Committee on Novel Foods and Processes (ACNFP) will have specific responsibility for monitoring the safety aspects of genetically modified foods.

What about the impact of genetically modified crops on the environment?

Genetically modified organisms may not be released into the environment without approval. In the UK, the environmental aspects of new foods are regulated through an EU directive. Initial laboratory work is controlled by the Health and Safety Executive (HSE) who consult the Advisory Committee on Genetic Modification (ACGM). Advice on the development of these crops is given to the government by a scientific committee, the Advisory Committee on Releases to the Environment (ACRE).

Several hundred field trials have been approved in the UK. Before approval for these trials can be given, a strict environmental risk assessment must be carried out by the Department of the Environment (DETR), and approval has to be given by the Secretary of State. Approval to grow the crops commercially will not be given until the trials have been completed and the regulators are satisfied.

In other parts of the world, such as Canada and the USA, genetically modified crops are now grown extensively after the regulatory authorities there concluded that there was no threat to the environment. Many thousands of field trials with genetically modified crops have taken place worldwide since 1987 and in 1999 commercially grown plants covered an area of 39.9 million hectares.

Could the new genes in these crops be passed on to other plants?

The question of the transfer of genes from genetically modified crops to other plants is considered carefully by the regulators. They have accepted that there is no greater risk of this happening than exists with the conventional crops grown in this country at present. Our extensive experience of genetically modified crops which are grown elsewhere in the world supports this view.

Is Monsanto involved in commercial genetics other than food bio-technology?

Monsanto is currently involved only in agricultural biotechnology. This includes techniques for the transfer of genetic material or characters between plant species or between micro-organisms and plants.

Such developments are generally regarded as an extension of plant breeding, but which allow more precise transfer of single traits or characters than the more random nature of cross-pollination.

We are not at present involved in any work with human genetics, or in the use of human genes. Neither are we involved in work with animal genetics in relation to animal breeding.

What is Monsanto's overall safety and environmental record?

Monsanto has an exemplary safety and environmental record, and we also have a policy of openly publishing our performance in these areas. We produce an Environmental Annual Review, in which we publish full details of our emissions and programmes to reduce them, as well as employee health and safety data.

In the 1980s we began a programme to reduce air emissions by 90 per cent, a goal we achieved in 1992. Since then we have set new targets for further reductions in all emissions by 70 per cent, with an ultimate goal of 'zero impact'.

What about consumer information?

Labelling helps consumers decide what they buy. Decisions about the labelling of foods containing ingredients from genetically modified crops are made by the European Union and the UK food industry labels many of these foods.

In order to help improve public understanding of modern biotechnology and genetic modification, the food industry in this country is working to keep consumers better informed. Public information is a priority and we at Monsanto are working to achieve this through a variety of different approaches.

- The above information is an extract from Monsanto's web site which can be found at www.monsanto.com

Genewatch

77% of the public believe there should be a ban on growing genetically engineered crops and food in Britain

The conclusive results of a new MORI poll indicate that the vast majority of the British public are currently opposed to the growing of genetically engineered crops in this country – the questions, results and poll technique are below.

Commissioned by Genewatch, the independent organisation which monitors development in genetic engineering, the MORI poll shows that 77% want a ban on the growing of such crops until their impacts have been more fully assessed. A similar number (73%) are concerned that genetically engineered crops could interbreed with natural, wild plants and cause genetic pollution.

The MORI poll also reveals that 61% of the public do not want to eat genetically modified foods (an 8% increase since a similar MORI poll was conducted in December 1996) and 58% of the public oppose the use of genetic engineering in the development of food (a 7% increase on 1996).

'How much more evidence does the Government need that the public do not want genetically engineered foods and that this opposition is increasing?' said one GeneWatch Director, Dr Sue Mayer. 'Until now, the Government has taken

61% of the public do not want to eat genetically modified foods – an 8% increase since a similar MORI poll was conducted in December 1996

little account of public opinion and has been complacent about the risks of introducing genetically engineered crops.'

From next year, herbicide-resistant oilseed rape could be the first genetically engineered crop to be grown commercially in Britain. A GeneWatch report, *Genetically Engineered Oilseed Rape: Agricultural Saviour or New Form of Pollution?*, to be published tomorrow, concludes that new research casts doubts on previous safety assessments and that serious damage could be done to the environment and farming.

Public rejection of genetically engineered foods could have serious consequences for food producers and retailers, who would be forced into an increasingly difficult search for products which could be guaranteed to be non

Public attitudes towards genetic engineering

Commissioned by Genewatch, the independent organisation which monitors developments in genetic engineering, this MORI poll shows that 77% want a ban on the growing of such crops until their impacts have been more fully assessed. A similar number (73%) are concerned that genetically-engineered crops could interbreed with natural, wild plants and cause genetic pollution. The poll also reveals that 61% of the public do not want to eat modified foods (an increase of 8% since a similar MORI poll conducted in December 1996) and 58% oppose the use of genetic engineering in the development of food (a 7% increase on 1996).

MORI asked: Genetic engineering makes it possible to artificially change the genetic make-up of, for example, plants, animals and micro-organisms (bacteria etc.). The changes made to those are maintained in future generations of the same plants, animals and micro-organisms. In the food industry, this technique has already begun to be used. There are, for example, genetically-engineered soya beans and maize. Modifying the genetic make-up through genetic engineering causes for example, beer to ferment faster, cheese to mature quicker, pigs to grow larger, makes grain immune to pests and tomatoes age more slowly. Supporters of genetic engineering in the food sector are expecting benefits such as more breeding techniques, better products and more efficient production methods. Critics are afraid of immeasurable health and ecological risks, like the creation of organisms resistant to disease. The EU is discussing labelling of food that is produced using genetic engineering.

Q 1. Thinking of genetically modified food or food derived from genetic engineering, what is your opinion towards the development and introduction of such food. Would you say you . . . ?

	1996 %	1998 %	Change %
Support it to a great extent	6	6	0
Support it slightly	25	16	-9
Neither support it nor oppose it	16	15	-1
Oppose it slightly	24	21	-3
Oppose it to a great extent	26	37	+11
Don't know	2	5	+3

Q 2. To what extent do you agree or disagree with this statement: 'I personally would be happy to eat genetically modified food'?

	1996 %	1998 %	Change %
Strongly agree	5	5	0
Tend to agree	22	21	-1
Neither agree nor disagree	17	10	-7
Tend to disagree	23	24	+1
Strongly disagree	30	37	+7
Don't know	2	3	+1

Q 3. Last November, the French government announced a ban on the growing of genetically-engineered crops in France until there has been public debate on whether they are safe and whether there is public support for genetically-engineered foods. At present, there is no such ban on the growing of genetically-engineered foods in this country. To what extent do you agree or disagree that the British Government should announce a similar ban on the growing of genetically-engineered foods in Britain until their impact has been more fully assessed?

Strongly agree	51%	Tend to disagree	9%
Tend to agree	26%	Strongly disagree	2%
Neither agree nor disagree	9%	Don't know	3%

Q 4. If genetically-modified plants (such as oilseed rape and sugar beet) come into contact with natural, but related plants in the wild, it is possible for them to breed, transferring the genetically modified material to the wild. How concerned are you, if at all, that genetically modified plants may come to breed with wild, natural plants in this way?

Very concerned	38%	Not at all concerned	6%
Fairly concerned	35%	Don't know	7%
Not very concerned	14%		

Technical note: MORI interviewed 950 adults aged 15+ face-to-face, in home, between 6-8 June 1998 throughout Great Britain. Data have been weighted to reflect the national profile. Trend information has been included from a MORI /Greenpeace International poll: 1,003 interviews among adults aged 15+ were conducted by telephone between 13-15 December 1996. Data have been weighted to reflect the national profile.

genetically engineered. Farmers could be faced with major problems from genetic pollution and uncontrollable herbicide-resistant weeds. 'In fact, the only people who are likely to benefit are the huge multinational companies which are developing the crops,' says Dr Mayer. 'The Government should not be rushed into introducing this new technology but should listen to its electorate and declare an immediate halt to the commercial exploitation of genetically engineered crops until the whole issue has been properly evaluated.'

About Genewatch

Genewatch is an independent organisation concerned with the ethics and risks of genetic engineering. It questions how, why and whether the use of genetic technologies should proceed and believes that the debate over genetic engineering is long overdue.

Genewatch's Director, Dr Sue Mayer, has been involved in monitoring developments in genetic engineering for eight years and was Director of Science at Greenpeace UK from 1990 to 1995. She is co-author of *Uncertain World, Genetically modified organisms, food and public attitudes in Britain* published in 1997.

© MORI/Genewatch

Doctors call for GM food ban to ease public fears

By Celia Hall,
Medical Editor

Leading doctors issued a demand today for an indefinite moratorium on the planting of genetically modified crops because of public concern and the lack of scientific evidence on their long-term safety.

A report from the British Medical Association says: 'As we cannot yet know whether there are any serious risks to the environment or human health, the precautionary principle should apply.' This is the first time that a leading medical organisation has commented on GM foods.

The BMA's tough recommendations include the call for a ban on the planting of crops resistant to antibiotics because of the possible implications for antibiotic resistance in humans. The report says it is 'essential' that testing for potential allergic reactions to genetically modified foodstuffs should be improved.

'We felt strongly that there should be a cautious approach,' said Prof Sir William Asscher, chairman of the BMA Board of Science, which produced the report. 'Our first anxiety is that there is no turning back once you have allowed something into the environment. If there is some adverse effect, that is it: it will be out there.'

The report, *The Impact of Genetic Modification on Agriculture, Food and Health,* says: 'The BMA believes that the current public mistrust of science, expert opinion and agriculture, following the BSE crisis, cannot be underestimated. Scientists, farmers and politicians have much work to do to re-establish public trust.'

The report says that the public must be better informed about testing sites for GM crops and calls for prominent displays of locations in local newspapers. It says that all food containing genetically modified material should be clearly labelled. This would help in maintaining a watch on health by making it easier to track any group of people that had suffered some adverse effect.

The statement concludes: 'Nothing in life is free of risk. When something is judged to be "safe", it merely falls within acceptable limits of risk.' It calls for the 'rigorous assessment' of any applications from companies to grow GM crops in trials and says that evidence from the United States of the environmental safety of such crops may not be applicable in Europe.

'Nothing in life is free of risk. When something is judged to be "safe", it merely falls within acceptable limits of risk'

Monsanto, the biotechnology company that leads the field in the global development of GM crops and foods, rejected the BMA's assertion that there was insufficient evidence to proceed. Tony Coombes, a spokesman for the company, said: 'How much more regulation does the BMA want? GM crops and GM foods are the most highly regulated novel products available.

'The regulatory system in this country is being copied throughout the world. We disagree very strongly with the BMA's assertion that there is insufficient evidence to inform decisions on GM foods.'

Campaigners said they were delighted by the BMA's statement. Charles Secrett, director of Friends of the Earth, said: 'It confirms precisely the points we have made throughout this debate. Extensive research needs to be done and no commercial licensing of GM crops can take place until this research has been completed. That will take at least five years.'

Doug Parr, the director of Greenpeace, said the Prime Minister should now listen to the voice of British doctors and ban GM foods. 'Tony Blair should do what the BMA says and stop this genetic experiment. This is the nation's doctors sensibly calling for a moratorium on further genetic experiments on the public at large.'

© Telegraph Group Limited, London 1999

Genetic science hailed by Blair

Genetic modification will be the revolutionary science of the 21st century, according to Tony Blair. Writing in *The Telegraph* today, Mr Blair delivers a spirited defence of the Government's refusal to bow to demands for a three-year blanket ban on commercial growing of GM crops.

In his first detailed response to the furore which has engulfed the Government, the Prime Minister makes it clear that he will not be pushed around by pressure groups and the media. He likens the deluge of adverse publicity and protests from environmental campaigners on GM foods to standing in front of a stampede. He said: 'It is never a nice business. But occasionally it has to be done.'

His article comes a day after five Cabinet ministers issued a letter to all MPs seeking to reassure the public over GM foods. It will be seen as a further sign that the Government has been losing the public relations battle and feels it needs to start a counter-offensive.

The Prime Minister accuses parts of the media and the Conservatives of conducting 'an extraordinary campaign of distortion and misinformation' about GM foods. 'Anyone who has dared to raise even the smallest hand in protest is accused of being either corrupt or Dr Strangelove.'

But Mr Blair reserves his strongest criticism for the Conservatives, who have taken the lead in Parliament in calling for a moratorium of three to five years on commercial planting of GM crops.

He says that the three GM foods currently on sale were licensed by the Tories before the election. Since coming to power, Labour has insisted on labelling for GM food, reversing the previous government's position. He said: 'The position of the Conservatives on this whole issue, with some

*By George Jones,
Political Editor*

honourable exceptions, has been so opportunistic and hypocritical as to beggar belief.'

He also accuses the Tories of waging war on Lord Sainsbury, the science minister, by calling for him to resign because of his former business links with the development of GM food. The Conservatives, he says, are using a 'peculiarly unpleasant personal attack' as a substitute for serious opposition. Mr Blair insists that the Government is motivated by a desire to 'get it right'. The safety of consumers is paramount, but people should also be aware of the risks of banning GM foods or crops without any proper evidence to support that decision.

He said: 'I am no scientist, but those who are make what seems to me a compelling case that biotech, the human genome project and genetic modification in its various forms will be the revolutionary science of the 21st century, as important as the computer was for the late 20th century. There is no scientific evidence on which to justify a ban on GM foods and crops.'

To ban products that independent scientific advisers had told the Government were safe would send a 'negative message' to the whole biotech industry in Britain that its future would be governed not by evidence but by media scares, he says.

Mr Blair says the GM controversy has taught him the importance of the Government standing firm and not yielding to an orchestrated barrage. On such an issue ministers need to be guided by good science, 'not soundbites and scaremongering', and should resist the 'tyranny of pressure groups'.

Downing Street also used the Internet in an attempt to put its case. The No 10 website last night gave detailed responses to reports over recent days, ranging from allegations that families were being used unwittingly as guinea pigs for GM foods, to allegations that the Government had stifled publication of scientific reports. It states: 'The GM debate of recent days has been characterised by hype, media myth and hysteria.'

© *Telegraph Group Limited, London 1999*

What's wrong with genetic engineering?

Information from Friends of the Earth

Health concerns

The health effects of eating genetically engineered foodstuffs are, as yet, unknown. Are we prepared to consume these products and wait and see? Recently a soybean containing genetic material from a Brazil nut caused allergies in individuals allergic to nuts. As a result the product was stopped before reaching the market. Will we know what is in our food and if we're allergic to it?

Austria and Luxembourg are currently resisting the import of genetically engineered maize which contains an antibiotic resistance gene left in from the laboratory stage. The countries are concerned that consumption of the maize will lead to an increased resistance to antibiotics in human and animal populations.

Environmental concerns

Releasing genetically engineered organisms into the environment represents 'genetic pollution'. There are long-held concerns about the transfer from genetically engineered crop plants to wild relatives to create 'superweeds' which could out-compete and disrupt the natural biodiversity of an area. At least ten genetically engineered crop plants are known to be capable of transferring their genetic qualities to wild plants.

Chemical farming

New uses for old pesticides is one sceptical view of the reason behind many genetically engineered crops. The majority of crops being designed for Europe are herbicide resistant thus maintaining farmers' dependence on chemicals.

Not by chance, Monsanto manufacture the herbicide 'Round-Up', allowing the company to sell farmers not just the genetically engineered seed e.g. soya but also the herbicide it is resistant to. Monsanto's herbicide Round-Up could not previously have been used on soya plants as it would have killed off the crop as well as the weeds. By developing a soybean resistant to the herbicide the profitability of the chemical is extended.

Is it really necessary?

The need for genetically engineered food is debatable. Is it not simply company profit margins demanding new products as the agrochemical era wanes under environmental pressure? Organic farmers are an agrochemical salesman's nightmare, as they don't need to buy chemical or genetically engineered products to grow good quality food. The facts are clear – sustainable, environmentally friendly farming would be far better for people's health and employment prospects.

Campaign aims

Friends of the Earth is campaigning for:

- a five-year moratorium on commercial planting of genetically engineered crops and imports of genetically engineered foods, to allow time for long-term fundamental research and proper public debate
- regulations controlling the release of genetically engineered organisms for trials and marketing to be tightened to protect farmers and the environment
- public consultation on all genetic engineering trials and experiments
- all genetically engineered crops to be fully segregated at harvest and tracked from field to supermarket shelf. This would allow a meaningful labelling scheme to be introduced
- a global ban on the use of gene technology which prevents seeds germinating (the so-called terminator technology)
- the Government's Advisory Committee on Releases to the Environment (ACRE) and Advisory Committee on Novel Foods and Processes to be reformed. And for the remit, and the range of their expertise, to be broadened.

GM food 'no worse than traditional plant crops'

By Charles Clover,
Environment Editor

Genetically modified foods are safe to eat according to all available evidence, the Government's chief medical and scientific advisers said yesterday in a report published alongside the Government's review of controls on the biotech industry.

Prof Liam Donaldson, the Chief Medical Officer, and Sir Robert May, the Chief Scientific Adviser, concluded in their report on the health implications of genetically modified foods that genetic engineering posed no more of a danger than mixing up genes through conventional plant breeding.

Jack Cunningham, the Cabinet Office minister, published the reports along with proposals for improving the regulatory framework of the biotech industry designed to repair public confidence. These included the creation of two new advisory bodies, the Human Genetics Commission and the Agricultural and Environment Biotechnology Commission. These will sit above advisory bodies which grant approvals to products and consider the ethics and potential risks of all new developments.

The new committees are expected to have a wide membership, including experts on ethics, environmentalists and gene scientists, and are due to be set up by the end of the year. Dr Cunningham rejected as too unwieldy the Royal Society's call for a single committee covering everything from medicine to agriculture.

He told the Commons that the regulatory system was 'generally sound, but needs to be developed and take a broader view'. Later he added: 'We are not prepared to be blown around hither and thither by alarmist "shock horror" reports which are not based on good science.'

In their report, Professor Donaldson and Sir Robert looked at the likelihood of GM crops producing substances which might be harmful to humans, or the chances of foreign DNA passing into human cells or bacteria in the gut.

The report said: 'We have considered the processes used in genetic modification in relation to events occurring in nature and in conventional plant breeding, and we conclude that there is no current evidence to suggest that the process of genetic modification is inherently harmful.' It added: 'We are reassured by the precautionary nature and rigour of the current procedures used to assess the safety of individual GM foods.'

Professor Donaldson and Sir Robert, however, added a cautionary rider: 'Nothing can be absolutely certain in a field of rapid scientific and technological development.' Genetic modification was a young science and there was a need to 'keep a close watch' on developments and to do further research.

The two advisers recommended that Government advisory bodies continued to monitor international developments in biotechnology closely. They called for the establishment of a national surveillance unit to watch for any unexpected outcomes in the population from the introduction of GM and other novel foods. The Government said it was discussing how to follow this recommendation.

Tim Yeo, Tory agriculture spokesman, said that the 'last five months of evasions, distortions and muddle have destroyed public confidence and dealt a fatal blow to a potentially important technology'. He welcomed the new advisory committees, however, as 'one step towards the rebuilding of public confidence'.

The British Medical Association welcomed the Government experts' statement, but said it still believed that their recommendations were not firm or robust enough to meet 'legitimate safety concerns'. Dr Vivienne Nathanson, head of health policy research at the BMA, however, said: 'They should be giving much stronger weight to the precautionary principle. We need more knowledge of the balance of risk and advantage before we embrace this new food technology.'

Doug Parr, campaign director for Greenpeace, said the measures announced by Dr Cunningham would not protect the British environment or save the Government: 'There could be health risks associated with the release of GMs into the food chain. The BMA has said so. Only today 96 per cent of the British public said they don't want GM food. No amount of presentation or spin will change this. There is no half-way house on this issue. You either go for the ban or you accept that GM technology, uncontrollable and unpredictable as it is, will riddle our world.'

Anna Bradley, director of the National Consumer Council, welcomed moves to strengthen the regulations governing the growth of GM crops. 'But we are very concerned that GM and conventional crops continue to be mixed at source in world markets. Mixed harvests make meaningful labelling of foods derived from GM sources impossible. That denies consumers the information they need to make effective choices.'

The Soil Association, the organic farming body, said the Government's review 'amounts to a total abdication of its duties to protect either the environment or the right of consumer choice'. The Government had mistakenly permitted a field-scale trial of GM rape in Worcestershire only six yards from a neighbouring organic crop.

Genetic engineering and human health

Genetic engineering (GE) involves the artificial insertion of a foreign gene into a host organism in an essentially random way. Extensive testing is needed to identify and propagate the tiny number of successes but there is always the chance that hazardous organisms could be unwittingly generated. There is also the chance that production of beneficial processes might be affected. There have been no long-term studies on the effects on animals and humans from eating genetically engineered organisms.

'The future responsibility of all farmers should be to use sound management and good husbandry to promote health rather than intervention with pesticides, drugs and genetic engineering to suppress disease.' (Patrick Holden, Director, Soil Association)

Health concerns

- There are concerns that genetically engineered Round-up Ready soya may contain higher oestrogen levels. No satisfactory tests have been undertaken.
- Some commentators fear that as genetically engineered bacteria and viruses increasingly escape into the environment from laboratories, new super-virulent pathogens may develop.
- There is evidence that DNA is not broken down as rapidly in the gut as previously supposed.

Antibiotic resistance in humans

Genetically modified plants often carry antibiotic-resistant marker genes to indicate to scientists where the modified genes rest in the plant.

- The use of antibiotic marker genes (an important tool in genetic engineering) may also prove to be dangerous.
- When a genetically engineered food plant containing an antibiotic-resistant marker gene is ingested by humans or animals, the resistant gene could transfer to bacteria in the gut, and be expressed by them, making them resistant to that particular antibiotic.

The creation of new toxins

- New toxins can be created unexpectedly with incalculable damage. In 1989 a new disease called EMS occurred in the US. It was linked to a batch of the food supplement Tryptophan that had been produced through genetically modified organisms – 37 died and 1500 people were disabled as a result of eating the contaminated product.

Unsuspected allergic reactions

- If proper labels do not accompany genetically engineered products, allergy sufferers may no longer be able to tell what is safe for them to eat.
- If a gene from a peanut is introduced into another food plant, this plant will then cause an allergic reaction in people who are allergic to peanuts.
- A brazil nut gene inserted into soya resulted in a reaction in people allergic to nuts.

Genetic engineering and the Soil Association

The Soil Association believes that genetic modification has no place in the production of safe and healthy food. Organic farming systems aim to produce food with care for human health, the environment and animal welfare. This is not compatible with the use of genetically engineered crops. This position is shared by the organic movement worldwide.

Legislation recommendations

- A ban on the use of genetically engineered ingredients in human/animal foods.
- A ban on the commercial planting of genetically engineered crops in the UK.
- Tighter regulations governing the release of genetically engineered organisms into the environment.
- If there is no ban, then there must be stringent regulations for clear and informative labelling which identifies the inclusion of all genetically engineered ingredients or derivatives in food to protect the right of the consumer to choose.
- The above information is from the Soil Association web site which can be found at www.soilassociation.org

© The Soil Association

A question of breeding

As the media storm in Britain over GM foods entered its second week, the focus shifted from health to the environment. *New Scientist* reveals the latest research on the impact of GM crops on wildlife. But first, discover why conventional plant breeding is every bit as risky . . .

By David Concar and Andy Coghlan

It looks just like an ordinary oilseed rape plant, but farmers in Canada know it as 'Smart Canola'. Because it carries genes for resistance to two families of herbicides, the farmers can kill off every weed in sight, without fear of damaging their harvest.

The prospect of plants that could in effect conspire with farmers to produce chemically sterilised fields has sent Europe's conservationists into a flat spin. They have issued dire warnings about the perils of agricultural biotechnology and call for moratoriums on GM plantings. But Smart Canola is not quite what it seems. While European officials agonise over the pros and cons of growing GM crops, they could do little to stop farmers planting this oilseed rape. The reason: Smart Canola is not genetically engineered.

Scientists at Pioneer Hi-Bred in Des Moines, Iowa, used normal breeding and selection techniques to create Smart Canola. This involved screening thousands of naturally occurring variants for strains resistant to herbicides. The company rejects any suggestion that its crops will encourage farmers to sterilise their fields and thus harm wildlife. 'You don't just go out there and apply these chemicals randomly,' says company spokesman Tim Martin.

But because the crop is not genetically engineered, Martin's assertion would not need to be put to the test before the rape could be grown in Europe. The only trials required would be experimental plantings designed to evaluate its performance to confirm that it really is a novel variety. In fact, Pioneer has already made one application to market Smart Canola in Britain. This was turned down, but only because the yield was too low – a problem the company is confident it can solve.

Smart Canola is just one of several conventionally bred crops that could in theory pose the same environmental hazards as GM plants. And yet these crops would bypass rules compelling companies to show that their GM crops are unlikely to create environmental problems. Other plants that could slip through the net include maize and soya beans designed to resist the same herbicides as Smart Canola, also from Pioneer Hi-Bred.

David Robinson of the Scottish Crop Research Institute near Dundee, a member of the British Government's Advisory Committee on Releases to the Environment (ACRE), says existing legislation is plagued by a 'double standard' that defies reason. 'The idea that herbicide-resistant crops produced by genetic engineering are inherently more hazardous than ones produced by conventional techniques is simply nonsense,' he says.

This point is reiterated in a report from ACRE on GM crops and wildlife that was released last week. Headlines claimed that the document detailed a catalogue of environmental disasters waiting to happen, from genes escaping from GM crops to create superweeds to insect and bird populations already decimated by intensive farming being killed off by genetic engineering.

In fact, the report is an even-handed analysis of the risks and benefits of introducing the crops onto Britain's farmland. It's true that the conservation watchdog English Nature has called for a ban on commercial plantings of GM crops that are resistant to broad spectrum herbicides. It is worried that more farmland would be wiped clean of wild plants as a result. The ACRE report acknowledges these fears but also lists possible advantages. These include less need to till soil to control weeds, which could help stem erosion.

One of the document's more alarming observations has nothing to do with GM crops, however. 'Potential adverse effects,' it notes, 'may be just as likely to occur as a result of conventional plant breeding programmes.'

Martin takes a more positive view of ACRE's statements on the similarity between GM and conventional crops. 'I see it as affirmation that conventional breeding can work just as well,' he says.

But for environmentalists, the ACRE report carries a sobering message. While they concentrate on attacking GM crops, the plants' conventionally bred cousins could sneak into Europe through the back door.

Genetic engineering

The impact on environment and wildlife

Traditional pollution incidents, such as oil spillage, are containable and usually have a limited environmental impact. In most cases nature will recover in time and recolonise polluted areas. The release of genetically engineered organisms is an entirely different issue as they can reproduce themselves and become incorporated into the ecosystems.

Once genetically engineered organisms are released into the environment if a serious incident occurs it may be impossible to reverse. There are a number of problems that have already been experienced as a result of releasing genetically engineered organisms into the environment.

Genetically engineered (GE) crops may have unexpected effects on fragile ecological systems

- Monsanto's genetically engineered Round-up Ready crops which are resistant to glyphosate allow crops to be sprayed with impunity. Glyphosate is a broad spectrum herbicide which kills a wide range of wild plants as well as insects, birds, and other animals that depend on these plants for food and shelter.
- There have been a number of incidents where genetically engineered micro-organisms have killed beneficial soil fungi (*Advances in Applied Microbiology*, vol40, p237, 1995).
- Genetically engineered salt-tolerant crops could be produced commercially in marginal environments, like salt flats, which currently provide unique habitats for birds and other species.

Genetically engineered plants can kill beneficial insects as well as pests

- The death rate of lacewings (a food source for birds) was doubled when they were fed on plant-

eating larvae raised on genetically engineered maize.
- Rapeseed engineered to produce a natural insecticide has also been shown to kill not only the target pests – caterpillars and beetles – but also bees.
- Ladybirds eating aphids who had fed on genetically engineered potatoes were found to suffer from shortened life spans and reduced fertility

Genetically engineered plants cross with wild relatives

- French research has shown that genes which have been inserted into oilseed rape to confer resistance to herbicide can cross into wild weed populations.
- If herbicide tolerance is passed on to new hybrids, current herbicides would become useless to farmers and new more powerful brands would be required.
- Organic/conventional farmers wishing to grow non genetically engineered crops will be unable to guarantee they will remain free of GE pollution.
- Virus-resistant genes can be passed on to weedy relatives of crop plants with unpredictable effects on weed populations.

Genetic engineering for insect control encourages insects to become resistant, thus rendering the technology useless

- A number of commercial genetically engineered crops contain a gene from the soil bacteria Bt

(*Bacillus thuringiensis*, a product used by organic farmers as a natural form of pest control).
- These genes cause the plants to produce a natural toxin which is lethal to many caterpillars and grubs.
- Constant exposure to high levels of the toxin is likely to increase resistance among these pest species.
- The US Environment Protection Agency estimate that most pests targeted by genetically engineered Bt crops will build up resistance within 3-4 years.

Genetic engineering and the Soil Association

The Soil Association believes that genetic modification has no place in the production of safe and healthy food. Organic farming systems aim to produce food with care for human health, the environment and animal welfare. This is not compatible with the use of genetically engineered crops. This position is shared by the organic movement worldwide.

Legislation recommendations

- A ban on the use of genetically engineered ingredients in human/ animal foods.
- A ban on the commercial planting of genetically engineered crops in the UK.
- Tighter regulations governing the release of genetically engineered organisms into the environment.
- If there is no ban, then there must be stringent regulations for clear and informative labelling which identifies the inclusion of all genetically engineered ingredients or derivatives in foods to protect the right of the consumer to choose.

• The information above is from the Soil Association web site which can be found at www.soilassociation.org/ Alternatively, please see page 41 for their postal address details.

© The Soil Association

Regulation of GM crops

Information from the Food & Drink Federation

Whether or not consumers are prepared to accept the technology very much depends on their confidence in the regulatory process. So, what are the controls, and are they effective?

Current regulations

Tests in the laboratory

GM crops are subject to a number of stringent regulatory hurdles. Firstly the genetic modification is thoroughly tested in the laboratory, often for a number of years, to check that the proposed modification works with no adverse consequences. This is regulated by an EU Directive which is implemented in the UK as the Genetically Modified Organisms (Contained Use) Regulations. Those wishing to carry out tests have to register with the Health and Safety Executive (HSE). Certain tests are subject to a detailed notification which is reviewed by HSE as well as a number of Government departments and advisory committees.

Field trials

Field trials are governed by the EU's 'Deliberate Release' Directive which is implemented in the UK as the Genetically Modified Organisms (Deliberate Release) Regulations.

Those who wish to carry out field trials must submit an application to the Department of the Environment, Transport and the Regions (DETR). Rigorous conditions are laid down to ensure that these small-scale releases do not risk harm to the environment or human health. The application must describe the modification, and give details of the proposed release together with a full environmental risk assessment. It is then comprehensively reviewed by ACRE to identify any possible risks to the environment. If further scientific information is needed ACRE will order research to be carried out; for example, it has requested extra research into the potential risks of GM insect-resistant crops to beneficial insects. Membership of ACRE now includes experts in ecology, biodiversity and farming practice.

Consents to grow commercial crops

The next step is to grow and market the GM crop on a commercial scale. This requires an application to market the GM plant which is reviewed both at national level and by the other Member States of the EU. In the UK applications are reviewed by DETR, ACRE, MAFF (the Ministry of Agriculture, Fisheries and Food), ACNFP (the Advisory Committee on Novel Foods and Processes) and COT (the Committee on Toxicity of Chemicals in Food, Consumer Products and the Environment). Where a particular pesticide will be applied to a GM crop, separate approval for the pesticide is required by ACP (the Advisory Committee on Pesticides), which in itself is a lengthy process. Clearance to grow GM crops commercially for food consumption has not yet been granted in the UK.

Critics of the current system

Many critics of the regulatory process focus on the advisory committees. Some object to the presence on them of representatives of the companies that own the technology. Despite assurances that these members are subject to strict rules which prevent them from participating in decisions that affect their interests, many feel that their presence alone gives rise to bias. In contrast, others point out that industrial representatives are needed as they are often the recognised experts. The perceived lack of

What about . . . a moratorium?

Much has been written about the perceived risks of GM technology and there have been many calls for a 'moratorium' on further research. Among those calling for a moratorium different people have different views as to what should be stopped. Some want all tests, even those in the laboratory, to be halted; others want only to delay wider-scale growth of GM crops for commercial use.

Supporters of the technology point out that some adverse results are to be expected in laboratory experiments. The whole point of research is to carry out such experiments in the confines of the laboratory and, learning from the results, establish procedures and systems to minimise risks in the field.

Thereafter, it is only through field trials, and then larger farm-scale trials, that the safety or otherwise of the technology can be determined.

Globally, 25,000 field trials of GM crops have been carried out so far with no significant adverse consequences. Supporters of GM technology argue that a moratorium on UK testing would mean that we would fall behind in developing a technology which is widely accepted elsewhere in the world. Others take the view that our fragile environment is too precious to be put at risk, however remote that risk might be.

• The above information is an extract from *GM crops & the Environment – Benefits & Risks* produced by the Food & Drink Federation. See page 41 for address details.

sufficient and appropriate consumer and environmental appointees on the committees is also a concern.

Another issue is monitoring. No test can ever fully replicate real life. With any novel food, new medicine or any other invention, no one can predict for certain what effect it will have when widely used. The same is true for GM crops. For this reason many interest groups advocate that GM crops should be closely monitored to assess their impact on the environment, even after the regulatory hurdles have been overcome and consents have been granted.

• The above information is an extract from GM *crops & the Environment – Benefits & Risks* produced by the Food & Drink Federation. See page 41 for address details. Also visit their web site at www.foodfuture.org.uk

Gone with the wind

Will buffer zones stop genes spreading to nearby crops? By Andy Coghlan

Pollen blown from large fields of genetically modified oilseed rape remains fertile over greater distances than expected, say British botanists. Their results could prompt a review of rules governing the size of the 'buffer' zones between transgenic and natural plants as the pollen fertilised plants after travelling twice the current buffer distance demanded in Britain.

Environmentalists have warned of dire consequences if genes that make crops resistant to herbicides spread to weeds. And organic farmers fear losing their status if their crops are pollinated by nearby transgenic plants. Such worries have already provoked one court case in Britain.

To see how far live pollen could spread, Jeremy Sweet and Euan Simpson of the National Institute of Agricultural Botany in Cambridge studied a 9-hectare plot of transgenic oilseed rape. The rape was resistant to glufosinate, a weedkiller made by AgrEvo of Frankfurt.

At various distances from the plot, the investigators grew male-sterile rape plants. Oilseed rape frequently self-fertilises, but because they make no pollen themselves, male-sterile plants are much more likely to be fertilised by airborne pollen. 'There's no competition, so they accept anything that's flying around,' says Simpson.

Afterwards, the researchers screened seeds produced by the male-sterile plants to see what proportion were resistant to glufosinate. Any resistant seeds must have been produced by plants cross-fertilised by genetically modified pollen blown on the wind.

Simpson and Sweet presented their results this week at a conference on gene flow and agriculture at the University of Keele in Staffordshire. Even at sites 400 metres away from the transgenic plots, as many as 7 per cent of the seeds were herbicide resistant. 'That is quite high,' says Simpson.

At 100 metres, between 8 and 28 per cent of the seeds were resistant. However, Simpson stresses that by using male-sterile plants, he and Sweet have examined a 'worst-case scenario'. 'Research has shown that you can get significant cross pollination at up to 50 metres, but there ought not to be anything to worry about beyond that,' say Simpson.

According to the existing British rules, experimental plots of transgenic oilseed rape must be grown at least 200 metres from unmodified crops. In earlier experiments, he and his colleagues examined 8,000 seeds from normal rape plants growing up to 150 metres from a field of transgenic rape, but found none with seeds that became herbicide resistant through cross-pollination. 'Fertile plants are a lot less likely to be fertilised by incoming pollen,' says Simpson.

This year, the researchers will repeat their experiments replacing half of the male-sterile plants with normal plants. 'We're putting both out so we can get a comparison,' says Simpson.

Test of the revolution

Mark Avery and David Gibbons, from the RSPB, argue that farm trials must be scientifically rigorous if they are to be a credible response to the worries surrounding GM technology

The RSPB's position is clear: we oppose the commercial growing of genetically modified (GM) crops until and unless they pass stringent tests. In contrast, the government's position is confused. Ministers have admitted that there is no pressing need for GM crops, have admitted concerns about environmental impacts of GM crops and yet have also said that they are keen to see them grown.

The government is funding farm-scale trials to measure the environmental impact of GM crops and yet it may allow commercial release of these same crops before the trials are completed.

Why should we worry about these new crops? GM crops currently being considered for UK release are modified to tolerate powerful broad-spectrum herbicides. Herbicides have probably played a major role in the drastic decline of farmland wildlife, particularly in the decline of such birds as the corn bunting (74% decline in population since 1972) and grey partridge (78%).

Herbicides are designed to destroy the weeds on which other wildlife depends. Farmland bio-diversity has already suffered enormously under intensive agriculture; herbicide-tolerant GM crops could make things even worse. The escape of genes into wild plants or neighbouring crops is almost inevitable if GM crops are grown on a large scale.

The wider arguments against commercial planting of GM crops in the UK are strong. Consumers don't want GM foods and supermarkets are removing them from their shelves. Without a market, farmers will not grow these crops and they're asking who will be liable should non-GM and organic crops be contaminated. Chartered surveyors say that farmland on which GM crops are grown could drop in value.

If the government decided to reverse its wish to see GM crops in the UK, then the farm-scale trials would be redundant and few would shed a tear. However, senior members of the government seem determined to press ahead with the introduction of GM crops.

Despite, or because of, the RSPB's serious and publicly-voiced concerns about GM crops, coupled with our track-record in studies of farmland ecology, we were invited on to the steering group overseeing these evaluations. The RSPB concluded that scientifically rigorous trials were the only reliable and responsible means of finding answers to the legitimate concerns that surround GM technology.

> *Nothing is more likely to stop GM crops being commercially planted in the UK than evidence that this would cause more environmental harm than current crop management*

Despite extensive media coverage of 'trial-trashing', the trials have not started in earnest. The steering group has met only once and the details of the trial design are not yet fully developed. The relatively few test fields planted so far will inform the design of the study but are not part of the trials themselves. So there is still everything to play for.

Nothing is more likely to stop GM crops being commercially planted in the UK than evidence that this would cause more environmental harm than current crop management. Unfortunately, this creates a real dilemma which we have had to face – the only way to measure the harm is, potentially, to cause some of it. But the harm must be minimised and we can foresee situations where we would withdraw our support for the trials.

So, the RSPB's support is in no way unconditional. We want assurance that the trials will be scientifically rigorous and, in particular, that the farms selected for trials are truly representative of UK agriculture. The trials must address all the important environmental issues including gene flow and herbicide use.

The trials' steering group has stated that meaningful results from the trials will not be available for at least three years.

Bizarrely, the government has maintained that it will consider granting commercial consent as early as next year. We repeat the RSPB's call for the government to ensure that there is no commercial planting of GM crops unless the trials give them a clean bill of health.

A potent reason for ensuring proper assessment of these crops is that many more are in the pipeline; insect-resistant crops, GM grasses and trees, and others. We face a potentially massive agricultural revolution. A stronger regulatory framework is therefore essential to minimise the environmental damage. If the trials reveal environmental problems then the government should ban the relevant GM crops permanently.

• Mark Avery is a member of a government working group examining how the regulatory system could take better account of the risks to biodiversity posed by GM crops. David Gibbons is on the scientific steering group overseeing the farm-scale trials of GM crops.

© The Guardian
August, 1999

Genetically modified organisms

Information from English Nature

Over the past 18 months GMOs have been the subject of much public debate. English Nature has had a high profile within the debate and maintained its position throughout. Following is the text from *Genetically Modified Organisms – English Nature's view*, a question-and-answer leaflet which clearly explains English Nature's position with regards to genetically modified organisms and the environment, which we hope you will find useful.

What is English Nature's role in relation to genetic modification of crops?

English Nature is the Government's statutory adviser on wildlife and natural features. As well as declaring and managing National Nature Reserves and notifying and promoting effective management of Sites of Special Scientific Interest, we monitor developments which may affect wildlife and advise on how any damaging effects might be avoided. This advice is based on over 40 years of practical experience, coupled with in-depth scientific knowledge. English Nature is committed to maintaining and enhancing biodiversity and natural heritage – our wealth of wildlife.

Are GMOs harmful to the environment?

The answer is that they may or may not be, we do not yet know. Given this uncertainty, and the possibility that serious harm could result if we get things wrong, we must exercise great care if any commercial releases are to be allowed. We know that the effects on wildlife of agricultural intensification over the last 40 years have been harmful, and GMO technology could be the next agricultural revolution – a revolution as far-reaching as the development of DDT.

Potential risks include:

- the direct toxicity of GM crops to wildlife (e.g. Bt crops to butterflies and moths). Recent American research indicates that butterfly survival rates can be adversely affected by GM pollen;
- the transfer of genes to native species either deliberately or inadvertently. The creation of herbicide-resistant grasses uncontrollable by herbicides could result in traditional flower-filled hay meadows being overrun;
- the potential for changes in agricultural methods enabled by GM crops. Fields of herbicide-resistant crops could be sprayed at the growing stage, eliminating all weeds on which wildlife relies for shelter and food. This would pose a particular threat to such typical farmland birds as skylarks.
- Even though biotechnology could be used to benefit wildlife, there are no incentives for industry to produce such crops and no mechanisms in place to ensure that new crops are used in ways which protect and benefit wildlife.
- There are at least 25 research projects currently under way in the UK which are investigating the effects of GM crops on the environment.

What is English Nature's position on commercial growing of GM crops?

English Nature is not opposed to genetic modification as a plant breeding technique, but is concerned about widespread release of certain GM crops. Our advice is that there should be a breathing space of at least three years (preferably five) before the commercial release of GM herbicide-tolerant (HT) and insect-resistant (IR) crops to allow time for research into their effects on biodiversity to be completed and assessed.

Has any research been done on the effects of herbicide-tolerant (HT) and insect-resistant (IR) GM crops on the environment?

We are not aware of any field research done either in Europe or in the US on the effects of growing these crops on biodiversity. There are a few laboratory-based studies which raise questions about adverse effects on wildlife.

We can make predictions about the effects on biodiversity from linking agricultural research on the efficiency of GM crop systems with what we know about the effects of 'conventional' agricultural intensification on biodiversity. For example we know that the herbicide methods used with new GMHT crops remove about 98% of all weeds. It is very difficult to achieve this efficiency with conventional weed-removal systems. There is a lot of research on the effects of highly intensive farming on birds, insects and plants which proves that highly efficient herbicide (and insecticide) systems cause serious damage to biodiversity. We fear that commercial adoption of GMHT crops and the impact of associated herbicides and insecticides will cause further severe declines in farmland biodiversity. In other words, it is at least as bad as current intensive systems, and under some circumstances, worse. We need to learn the lessons from the past 30 years of increasing agricultural intensification to set the framework for this new technology.

Who is doing research?

Most of the research on the effects of growing GM crops on biodiversity is being sponsored by DETR and MAFF, although some is also being funded by the biotechnology industry. Current research programmes cover only a small part of what needs to be done to ensure ecological safety. English Nature has presented the Government with a list of suggested additional research.

How long will the research take?

At least three years. The earliest that most of these ecological research projects will be completed by is 2002. It will take a further year for the results of various projects to be

integrated and assimilated by the regulatory system. That is why we have called for a delay in the commercial release of GMHT and IR crops of at least three, preferably five, years.

Won't GM crops reduce the amount of pesticides and therefore benefit wildlife?

It is not always the amount of pesticide which damages wildlife, but the type used and the timing of application.

Conventional weed treatments using pre-emergence and selective herbicides should achieve success early in the season but leave weeds later on. The herbicides used on GMHT crops would be broad-spectrum chemicals such as glyphosate (e.g. RoundupTM) and glufosinate (e.g. LibertyTM) which, when applied during the growing season, kill almost all weeds in the field. We know that on very intensive farms, conventional weed treatments are very damaging to biodiversity, but many farms are not so intensive and tolerate relatively weedy fields.

In the USA, treatment with broad spectrum herbicides applied to growing GM crops appears to have increased cases of spray drift damage to adjoining non-GM crops. If these methods are transferred to the UK, we fear further damage to hedgerows and field margins which provide the most valuable remaining refuge for wildlife in the farmed landscape.

Will genes from GM crops spread to wild plants?

Recent research from DETR and other information indicates that spread to native species is likely.

Some GM crops, such as maize and wheat, have no wild relatives in England and it is very unlikely that genes from these could spread to wild plants. Others, such as oilseed rape and sugar and fodder beet are closely related to a number of wild plants. Recent research shows that GM pollen spreads to these plants and that fertile hybrids are formed. We do not yet know what the impact of these hybrids could be on wildlife and agriculture – will some become aggressive weeds invading either farmland or natural habitats? Will the hybrids prove 'fitter' than their wild relatives and replace them? Will some hybrids be insect-resistant, denying wild insects their food and leading to declines in insect-eating birds?

We do not know the answers to these questions. Some research has recently been started in Europe to investigate the impact of gene escape on biodiversity, and we do not want decisions to be taken before the results of the research are known.

These crops are widely grown in the USA. What is the effect on wildlife there?

The American situation is very different. In England, wildlife and farming share the countryside. In many parts of America, intensive farming and wildlife are sharply divided and zoned to the point of mutual exclusion. About 70% of land in the UK is farmed, in contrast to the US where around 35% is farmed. If we are to honour international biodiversity undertakings and conserve our native species, we must farm in ways which allow them to use the whole countryside. Transferring the industrialised farming of the US to the European landscape could have further devastating effects on our wildlife. In some areas such as East Anglia, northern France and parts of the Netherlands this has already happened and we have seen reductions of up to 75% in farmland bird populations over the past 25 years. English Nature wants to reverse this decline, and to see both a healthy agricultural economy and flourishing wildlife.

Is the regulatory regime for GMOs adequate?

Recent changes announced by Government should result in a regulatory and advisory structure which gives better control of GMOs, but there is much still to be done to incorporate testing for risks to biodiversity into the system. The forthcoming review of the European Directive governing release of GMOs (EC 90/220) is crucial to this process. It is important that the UK Govern-ment plays a leading role in the review, especially where potential effects on the environment are concerned.

Is the SCIMAC voluntary code of practice for GMHT crops enough to protect biodiversity?

The Code is very limited in its purpose and is not designed to protect biodiversity in the face of widespread release. It does not set out to protect wildlife within the crop and the field margins. Even if growers followed the Code to the letter, they could eliminate all wildlife from their fields. The Code is intended to protect the integrity of the supply chain and should not be seen as the solution to the biodiversity risks.

Should there be statutory control of growing GM crops?

Voluntary codes of practice in agriculture have rarely worked as intended. They failed for pesticides and for straw-burning, eventually being replaced by strong legislation. Biotechnology is such a powerful way of producing radically new crops that we believe statutory on-farm controls are essential.

What action is English Nature seeking?

- We are pressing Government and the biotechnology industry for a delay in commercial introduction of GMHT and IR crops until research is completed and results assimilated.
- We are calling for more ecological research to be started now.
- We are working to change the regulatory system to include much greater consideration of the potential effects of GM crops on wildlife.
- We believe that only statutory control of how GM crops are grown will ensure that wildlife is protected.

© English Nature Press Office
June, 1999

Food for the future

Judith Jordan says biotechnology is making crop production safer for the environment

The crops being evaluated, oil-seed rape and forage maize, which have been grown in North America for a number of years, have already undergone the necessary regulatory tests to assess food safety and are still undergoing other regulatory tests to determine their suitability and merit to UK agriculture. AgrEvo UK has been following government protocols to test all its products, including conventional agrochemicals and seeds derived from biotechnology.

The genetic modification currently being tested by AgrEvo UK is herbicide tolerant to one specific herbicide. The herbicide to which the forage maize and oilseed rape is tolerant is glufosinate ammonium. This active ingredient was first detected in the environment where it is produced as a by-product from a soil micro-organism and shown to exhibit herbicidal properties.

Glufosinate is rapidly degraded in the soil and water so that leaching is not a problem. Indeed, the degradation products of glufosinate are natural substances: phosphoric acid, carbon dioxide and water.

AgrEvo have marketed glufosinate ammonium since 1984 and it has been applied to over one million hectares in the UK, used in fruit and vegetable growing and arable farming for the control of weeds. It is a 'contact' herbicide, given that it can only control a weed when placed directly on to its green leaf.

Other types of herbicides commonly used are termed 'residual'. This is because they form a layer of active herbicide in the upper layers of the soil surface controlling weeds as they emerge, hence they are often applied before the germination of weed species.

Nearly 90% of forage maize in the UK is treated with a residual herbicide because there are very few contact herbicides that are safe to the crop and also it is a cost-effective option enabling season-long weed control from one application.

AgrEvo UK trials with herbicide tolerance have proved that weeds can be allowed to germinate, along with the crop, before they need to be controlled, allowing a natural environment for wildlife. The application of the herbicide is timed to enable weeds to be controlled just prior to when they would compete with and choke the crop. Forage maize readily forms a canopy some 5-6 feet high. A shade-tolerant canopy of smaller weeds, and its associated insect population, can therefore survive below.

We believe that biotechnology will enable crop production to be more environmentally friendly, with fewer, more benign chemicals applied, to provide higher quality, nutritious food as well as a plentiful and cost-effective food production system.

© The Guardian
August, 1999

Protecting the consumer interest

Genetically modified organisms

Genetically modified foods are transforming our food supply. No longer hi-tech foods of the future, they are already on supermarket shelves. The next few years will see most major food crops genetically modified making them easier to grow, cheaper to process and more attractive to consumers – or so it is claimed.

But these foods are being introduced against a background of public unease over food safety. A decade of food scares has eroded the public's confidence in the food industry and government. Concerns over the potentially unknown and long-term effects of genetic modification and the apparent ease with which these new foods and ingredients have entered the food chain – often without consumer knowledge – have reinforced public disquiet. Genetically modified soya, for example, could now be in approximately 60 per cent of processed foods, but no one can know for sure because US producers have mixed the genetically modified crop together with conventional soya. This has made accurate labelling very difficult and prevented consumers from exercising choice over whether or not they consume foods containing genetically modified ingredients.

The recent commercialisation of genetically modified soya and maize has also highlighted the extent to which large multi-national companies exercise a powerful influence over what we eat. Bio-technology companies were able to introduce products onto the market before a proper public debate about risks and benefits, and even prior to legislation to control their use. Genetically modified foods may provide potential benefits for consumers but in the meantime our research shows they are worried about the consequences if these foods prove not to be safe.

Striking the right balance between potential benefits and possible safety problems is not easy. The recent experience with BSE demonstrates that we cannot always anticipate potential risks to the consumer resulting from changes in food production. And although we cannot expect to have completely risk-free food, we should be able to have confidence in the way government assesses and regulates safety. But the law in this area is still trying to come to terms with the many uncertainties which remain and the fact that scientists do not themselves always agree on the risks posed by these new products. Despite these gaps in our knowledge, new products continue to be approved without any legal requirement to monitor the long-term implications for food safety or any rights of redress for the consumer if something should go wrong.

What are the public's concerns?

The Consumers' Association has been conducting consumer research into genetic modification since 1994, when the first product – a vegetarian cheese – was introduced by the Co-op. Since then we have tracked consumer attitudes towards the technology – in 1996 when genetically modified tomato purée was introduced, again in 1997 with the introduction of genetically modified soya and maize and more recently in 1998 when we were involved in a citizens' jury to consider the role of GM in food production.

Our research indicates that consumers' concerns cover a wide range of health, environmental, and ethical considerations including:

- lack of information about which foods have been modified, or how and for what purpose they have been modified;
- worries over the long-term consequences of genetic modification

THE SUPERMARKET GENOME PROJECT TRACKS DOWN THE GENES HIDING IN THE PRODUCTS ON THESE VERY SHELVES!!

— GENES THAT WILL IMPROVE YOUR SHELF-LIFE, RID YOU OF BOTHERSOME INSECTS, MAKE YOU RESISTANT TO POWERFUL AGRICULTURAL CHEMICALS …..

- lack of trust in government or industry over food safety;
- belief that the food industry will benefit most from genetic modification;
- a feeling amongst some that modifying plants and animals is unnatural;
- more consumers would be prepared to buy food from genetically modified plants than from genetically modified animals;
- the majority of consumers want modified foods to be clearly and fully labelled.

It is too early to say whether genetically modified foods will prove to be a miracle or a menace, but in the meantime Consumers' Association would like to see a new approach to genetic modification which acknowledges public concerns and puts consumer protection at the centre of public policy. Consumers' Association would like the following measures to be introduced:

New procedures for approving GMOs

- More research into the long-term implications for the environment and food safety is required in order to restore public confidence.
- Those advising the government should be able to take into account the wider impact of growing genetically modified crops on other areas of policy such as sustainable development, nature conservancy and chemical reduction.
- Government advisers should be drawn from a wider range of backgrounds and disciplines to ensure that public concerns are taken into account.
- Ethical concerns over the use of human genes in foods and the modification of animals should be considered during the approval of applications.
- Research into consumer attitudes towards genetic modification of animals and fish is required before market approval.
- Where there is uncertainty or gaps in knowledge a precautionary approach should be taken until such time as a rigorous risk assessment can be made.

New safety controls

- Long-term monitoring of the use of genetically modified foods should be a legal requirement.
- Genetically modified processing aids such as additives and enzymes are widely used but are not covered by the existing law. Given their impact, and their potential to cause harm, legislation on processing aids is required so that they are assessed for safety on the same basis as other genetically modified foodstuffs.
- In view of the world-wide problem of bacterial antibiotic-resistance, antibiotic-resistant marker genes should not be used when acceptable alternatives are available.
- Consumers should be given rights of redress under the EU's Product Liability Directive (the UK's Consumer Protection Act 1987) so they are legally protected if a genetically modified food causes harm.

Protecting the right to choose

- Segregation is fundamental to the principle of choice. The EU, UK government, retailers and manufacturers must ensure that growers segregate genetically modified crops.
- All foods or food ingredients that are derived by the use of genetic modification should be labelled. This would include foods and food ingredients where the genetically modified material is no longer intact or 'live'. This should be based on a requirement to ensure traceability.
- Standardised terminology is essential for labelling as consumers find the use of different wording on different products confusing. Our research shows 'genetic modification' to be the term most commonly understood which consumers want displayed 'up front'.
- Labelling should be supplemented by information on how and why food has been modified. Wherever possible, this information should be included on the packaging, or close to the product.
- Our research shows that consumers find symbols on packaging a useful way to identify particular processes or treatments. An internationally recognised symbol for use on products produced using genetic modification should be developed.
- Sensitive and reliable test methods should be developed and validated to confirm whether or not a product has been genetically modified.

The introduction of genetically modified foods, with minimal information or debate, has failed to inspire consumer confidence in the technology. Loopholes in the law have failed to provide consumers with adequate protection or meet their expectations. It is now time to redress the balance by putting consumers first – before our food undergoes substantial and irreversible changes.

© *Which On-line*

Genetic engineering and consumer choice

Information from the Soil Association

The precipitous introduction of genetically engineered (GE) foods has raised significant challenges to consumer choice. Under current labelling proposals it is estimated that 90% of foods containing ingredients from genetically engineered sources will not be required to be labelled as such.

Public opinion

- 61% of the British public said they do not want to consume genetically engineered ingredients according to a recent opinion poll. (MORI)
- 77% of the British public said they were opposed to the growing of genetically engineered crops in the UK. (MORI)
- 58% said supermarkets should cease stocking genetically engineered food.

The Government's position

- The Government have stated that they accept the right of the individual to choose whether or not to eat genetically engineered ingredients.
- The Government considers choice can be achieved through present labelling regulations.
- The current EU labelling Directive contains a number of deficiencies (e.g. additives such as lecithin, flavourings and processing aids which may contain GE ingredients are specifically excluded from the labelling scheme).

Impact on choice

- Due to the current labelling legislation consumers have lost their right to choose whether or not to eat products that contain genetically engineered ingredients.
- Religious groups may lose their right not to eat products that contain genes from certain animals (e.g. Muslims may unwittingly eat genes from a pig).
- Meat produced from animals fed on genetically engineered foods does not need to be labelled.
- Even organic foods which expressly prohibit the use of GE may not be able to claim to be GE free in the medium term due to the process of 'genetic pollution' – the spread of genes through cross-fertilisation.

The industry position

- Industry interests have lobbied fiercely to ensure weak labelling legislation governing food products containing genetically engineered ingredients.
- Recently a Nestlé executive admitted that it was no longer possible to make a claim that any food was GE free.

Genetic engineering and the Soil Association

The Soil Association believes that genetic modification has no place in the production of safe and healthy food. Organic farming systems aim to produce food with care for human health, the environment and animal welfare. This is not compatible with the use of genetically engineered crops. This position is shared by the organic movement worldwide.

Legislation recommendations

- A ban on the use of genetically engineered ingredients in human/animal foods.
- A ban on the commercial planting of genetically engineered crops in the UK.
- Tighter regulations governing the release of genetically engineered organisms into the environment.
- If there is no ban, then there must be stringent regulations for clear and informative labelling which identifies the inclusion of all genetically engineered ingredients or derivatives in foods to protect the right of the consumer to choose.

© The Soil Association

If we fear technology, we really fear ourselves

By Dr William Reville

The *Collins English Dictionary* defines technology as 'the total knowledge and skills available to any society for industry, art, science etc.' People generally feel uneasy about technology. We recognise that we are dependent on it but at the same time we feel in a vague way that we are in thrall to an alien influence.

In my opinion these widespread feelings are supported by two feet of clay. One foot is the alienation resulting from the general lack of understanding of the technical and scientific basis of our everyday technology. The other foot, which I will deal with in this article, is the mistaken idea that technology is an unnatural interloper into an otherwise natural world.

Technology is natural, and to fear technology is to fear ourselves. Tools are not unique to humans. Some animals use tools in hunting and some birds use tools in nest-building. Archaeology shows that mankind developed and used technology from the very beginning. Early men and women used clubs to hunt and warmed themselves by covering their bodies with animal skins. This early human technology may have developed by imitating nature, e.g. the bird which breaks a snail shell by banging it against a stone, but the subsequent human invention of improved tools distinguishes us from animals.

Man's earliest tools were simply extensions of the body. The arm was extended and strengthened by the club, the foot was hardened by the shoe, the skin was protected by clothes. Later technologies, such as the wheel and the bow, went far beyond simple imitation of nature but because they grew from human creativity they must be classified as natural.

Apart from facilitating labour and relieving burden the development of technology was also driven by a desire to achieve predictability.

For example, the earliest agriculture simply harvested whatever came naturally to hand.

But this provided a very unpredictable food supply and therefore humans developed the technology of agriculture – planting, fertilising and irrigating crops – in order to ensure reliable food supplies. Modern industrialised agriculture is still largely driven by the desire to ensure predictability of outcome.

Three stages can be recognised in the development of technology. The first is called the tool stage in which human energy is guided by human intelligence, such as the use of a wrench to tighten a nut. The second is the machine stage where non-human energy is guided by human intelligence, e.g. the pneumatic wrench. The third stage is the automated machine which uses non-human energy and directs its own activities, e.g. robots on a car assembly line.

Technology inexorably develops to the automated state. We are surrounded by innumerable examples – thermostatically controlled heating and cooling, telephone answering machines, automatic car transmissions and chokes, automated assembly lines etc. Automation is often portrayed as particularly unnatural and threatening to human freedom. However, there is nothing unnatural in the concept of automation. Most of the human body is automated – we breathe automatically, our hearts beat automatically, our guts constrict and dilate automatically etc.

Human psychology tends to fear that which it does not control. This is often to ignore the fact that many automated processes work more reliably and safely than technology that is under human control. For example, most aircraft accidents result from human error and not machine error. Most road accidents result from human error and not from malfunctioning cars. More domestic fires result from human error than from malfunctioning devices.

But the question of control should not be considered in isolation from the question of understanding. In many cases where the individual

feels he/she has no control over technology, it is also the case that he/she doesn't understand the technology either. Achieving an understanding would probably greatly ameliorate the unease felt over the lack of control. And residual (and understandable) fears about lack of control could be dealt with in many cases by providing a facility for manual intervention or override.

It also seems to be part of human psychology to look backwards with a rosy romantic eye and to look to the future with a wary and untrusting outlook. We tend to be uncritical of the 'good old days' before life became so 'mechanical' and before the environment became so 'polluted'. We gaze at a painting of a rustic village scene from a past century and idealise the simple healthy lifestyle.

We ignore the squalor, disease and deprivation that we know existed then but that isn't pictured in the cosy scene.

We even idealise past technology, such as the steam engine, as having a noble and unthreatening character compared with the technology of today, ignoring the fact that, in its time, the old technology was criticised in exactly the same fashion as is the modern technology now.

The analysis that underpins the philosophy of the Green Movement is heavily informed by a romantic view of the past and an antipathetic view of modern science and of science-based technology. The notion that technology is intrinsically unnatural is wrong and leads to a mindset that divides the world into 'goodies' and 'baddies'. This

occasionally degenerates into completely self-defeating actions such as the recent illegal vandalising of the Monsanto genetically modified beet experiment in west Cork.

Technology is no more unnatural than music, philosophy or any other product of the human intellect. Just as with these other activities, you can have good and bad technologies, and the process needs to be monitored. We have learned in recent decades that we are part of the natural environment and must also accept that technology is a natural product of human activity and a natural extension of the human capacity.

• William Reville is a senior lecturer in bio-chemistry and director of microscopy at UCC.

Genetically engineered food

Information from Greenpeace

If current trends continue, within a few years most of the foods we eat could be genetically engineered. Transnational corporations want us to believe that this food is safe, nutritious and thoroughly tested. Independent scientists, however, warn us that current understanding of genetics is extremely limited. They believe that this technology is flawed and carries inherent risks.

What is a gene?

All plants and animals contain millions of cells, each of which has a nucleus. Inside every nucleus there are strings of DNA, organised into structures called chromosomes. If all the DNA in the human body were unravelled it would reach the moon and back 8,000 times! Each cell normally holds a double set of chromosomes, one of which is inherited from the mother and one from the father. One set of chromosomes from each parent combines when the sperm fertilises the egg (in the case of animals) or pollen fertilises the ovum (in the case of plants). The cell formed after fertilisation divides into two identical copies,

each of which inherits this unique new combination of chromosomes. These embryonic cells then continue to divide and divide again. The inherited genetic material, carried in the chromosomes, is therefore identical in each new cell.

DNA is often described as a blueprint which contains all the essential information needed for the structure and function of an organism, and genes are described as the individual messages which make up the blueprint, each gene coding for a particular characteristic. Although this concept can be helpful as a tool for understanding, it runs the risk of reducing the organism to a machine, and viewing physiology as little different from a series of industrial processes. In reality, however, genes are very difficult to define and can only be understood within their context – a living organism.

No gene works in isolation. Genes are sequences of DNA which operate in complex networks that are tightly regulated to enable processes to happen in the right place and at the right time. This intricate network is informed and influenced

by environmental feedback in relationships that have been evolving over millions of years. According to Barbara McClintock, who won the Nobel Prize in 1983 for her pioneering work in the field of genetics, the functioning of genes is 'totally dependent on the environment in which they find themselves'.

What is genetic engineering?

In traditional forms of breeding, variety has been achieved by selecting from the multitude of genetic traits that already exist within a species' gene pool. In nature, genetic diversity is created within certain limits. A rose can cross with a different kind of rose, but a rose will never cross with a mouse. Even when species that may seem to be closely related do succeed in breeding the offspring are usually infertile. For example, a horse can mate with an ass, but the offspring, a mule, is sterile. These boundaries are essential to the integrity of any species.

In contrast to traditional breeding, genetic engineering involves taking genes from one species and inserting them into another in an

attempt to transfer a desired trait or character: for example, selecting a gene which leads to the production of a chemical with antifreeze properties from an arctic fish (such as the flounder) and splicing it into a tomato or strawberry to make it frost-resistant. It is now possible for scientists to introduce genes taken from bacteria, viruses, insects, animals or even humans, into plants.

It has been suggested that, because we have been modifying the genes of plants and animals for thousands of years, genetic engineering is simply an extension of traditional breeding practices. While it is true that the food crops we are eating today bear little resemblance to the wild plants from which they originated, it is clear that through this new technology organisms are being manipulated in a fundamentally different way.

How is this done?

There are a number of techniques in the genetic engineer's toolkit. Biochemical 'scissors' called restriction enzymes are used to cut the strings of DNA in different places and select the required genes. These genes are usually then inserted into circular pieces of DNA (plasmids) found in bacteria. The bacteria reproduce rapidly and within a short time thousands of identical copies (clones) can be made of the 'new' gene. There are now two principal methods which can be used to force the 'new' gene into the DNA of the plant that is to be engineered.

1. A 'ferry' is made with a piece of genetic material taken from a virus or a bacterium. This is used to infect the plant and in doing so smuggle the 'new' gene into the plant's own DNA. A bacterium called *Agrobacterium tumifaciens* which usually causes gall formation in plants is commonly used for this purpose. Or

2. The genes are coated onto large numbers of tiny gold pellets which are fired with a special gun into a layer of cells taken from the recipient organism, with any luck finding a hit somewhere in the DNA in the nucleus of the cells.

Genetically engineered (GE) animals and fish are produced by microinjection. Fertilised eggs are injected with new genes which will, in some cases, enter the chromosomes and be incorporated into the animal's own DNA.

Because the techniques used to transfer genes have a low success rate, the scientists need to be able to find out which of the cells have taken up the new DNA. So, before the gene is transferred, a 'marker gene' is attached which codes for resistance to an antibiotic. Plant cells which have been engineered are then grown in a medium containing this antibiotic, and the only ones able to survive are those which have taken up the the 'new' genes with the antibiotic-resistant marker attached. These cells are then cultured and grown into mature plants.

It is not possible to guide the insertion of a new gene with any accuracy, and this random insertion may disrupt the tightly controlled network of DNA in an organism.

Unpredictable effects

Current understanding of the way in which genes are regulated is extremely limited. Any change to the DNA of an organism at any point may well have knock-on effects that are impossible to predict or control.

- A gene coding for red pigment was taken from a maize plant and transferred into petunia flowers. Apart from turning white, the flowers also had more leaves and shoots, a higher resistance to fungi and lowered fertility.

The random insertion of a foreign gene may disrupt the tightly controlled network of DNA in an organism. The gene could, for example, alter chemical reactions within the cell or disturb cell functions. This could lead to instability, the creation of new toxins or allergens, and changes in nutritional value.

A piece of DNA taken from a virus or bacterium (called a 'promoter') is inserted along with the 'new' gene in order to 'switch it on' in its new host. Promoters, which often force genes to be produced at 10 to 1000 times normal levels, also have the potential to influence neighbouring genes. The promoter may, for example, stimulate a plant to produce higher levels of a substance which is harmless at low levels but which becomes toxic when present in higher concentrations.

- A yeast was genetically engineered for increased fermentation purposes. This led to the production of a metabolite called methyl-glyoxal in toxic and mutagenic concentrations.

Inadequate safety testing of genetically engineered (GE) food

Many people became aware of GE food for the first time in 1996 when soybeans grown in the US were genetically engineered by Monsanto to be resistant to their best-selling herbicide Round-up. Over 40% of the US soybean harvest is exported. When the first consignment of GE soya arrived in Europe, it was already mixed in with the conventional harvest. The American Soybean Association rejected calls to segregate the GE soya on the basis that it was 'substantially equivalent' to ordinary soya.

The theory of 'substantial equivalence' has been at the root of international guidelines and testing of GE food. According to this principle, selected chemical characteristics are compared between a GE product and any variety within the same species. If the two are grossly similar, the GE product does not need to be rigorously tested on the assumption that it is no more dangerous than the non-GE equivalent.

From a scientific standpoint, the use of 'substantial equivalence' as a basis for risk assessment is seriously flawed, and cannot be depended on as a criterion for food safety. Genetically engineered food may contain unexpected new molecules that could be toxic or cause allergic reactions. A product could not only be 'substantially equivalent', but even be identical with its natural counterpart in all respects bar the presence of a single harmful compound.

- In 1989, 37 people died in the United States after consuming a food supplement called L-tryptophan that had been produced from GE bacteria. It was regarded as 'substantially equivalent' and passed as safe for human consumption.

GE foods already on the market in the US include corn, soybeans, potatoes, squash, tomatoes, chicory and papaya as well as milk and other dairy products from cows treated with a genetically engineered growth hormone (rBST). A variety of enzymes produced from genetically engineered micro-organisms are used throughout the food processing industry. None of these foods have been subject to long-term safety studies or the kind of rigorous toxicological assessment that is applied to pharmaceuticals. Pharmaceuticals undergo up to 15 years of clinical trials which are still limited in their ability to assess unexpected problems; when pharmaceuticals are put on the market, 3% of them need to be withdrawn due to serious side-effects.

Public concern

Numerous surveys have been conducted around the world in order to monitor public attitudes towards GE food. In industrialised nations these have highlighted a discrepancy between government policy and public concern. With a few exceptions, governments have been keen to encourage the introduction of genetic engineering into the food supply. Opinion polls, however, have shown that most people would rather they did not have to eat it. Concerns fall into a number of categories:

Choice – consumers are worried that lack of segregation and labelling together with the fact that so many foods are being introduced will leave them unable to exercise free choice.

Health – people are becoming aware that there is a scientific basis to safety concerns about GE food, and are reluctant to replace food they know to be safe with food that might not be. A lack of trust in official assurances of safety, which has been exacerbated by the BSE crisis in the UK, has made people very suspicious of claims that there 'is no evidence of harm'.

Ethics – for some people the main issue is not whether genetically engineered food is safe or not, but the fact that it is unnatural and unnecessary. For some it offends deeply held principles about the relationship between humanity and nature.

Politics – international free-trade agreements are increasing the power of commercial interests and people are concerned that governments are being influenced by unelected bodies.

Profit – trade in GE food and crops is dominated by a handful of multi-national corporations such as Monsanto, Novartis, Zeneca, Aventis and DuPont. It is widely believed that these are the only beneficiaries of genetically engineered foods.

Environment – there is growing evidence that genetic engineering poses new risks to ecosystems, with the potential to threaten bio-diversity, wildlife and truly sustainable forms of agriculture. According to the research, it is the potential for long-term effects that most concerns people. Critics of the technology argue that once GE organisms have been released into the environment they may transfer their characteristics to other organisms and can never be re-called or contained.

Labelling

When people began to realise they were eating GE food without their knowledge or consent, there were immediate calls from consumer organisations around the world for mandatory labelling of all GE food.

On 27 May 1998, Codex Alimentarius (a UN body responsible for establishing international rules on food policy) rejected these calls in favour of a much more limited labelling regime that suited the food and genetic engineering industries. They used the argument of substantial equivalence to say that it would be discriminatory to enforce mandatory labelling of GE food, and suggested that this would constitute an illegal trade barrier. Mandatory labelling could mean that consumers would be able to boycott GE products, and that segregation would need to be introduced, potentially making GE food uneconomical for the food industry. Independent scientists have pointed out that GE food is in fact 'substantially different' from other food and that labelling is essential in order to be able to trace any health problems that may arise.

New EU legislation on partial labelling of GE soya and maize was introduced from September 1998. In Europe, GE soya is estimated to be present in about 60% of all processed food in forms such as vegetable oil, soya flour, lecithin and soya protein. GE maize can be found in about 50% of processed foods as corn, cornstarch, cornflour and corn syrup. Over 90% of these ingredients are excluded from the new labelling scheme.

So-called scientific arguments have been used by the food industry as a basis for refusing to label derivatives such as soya oil because most of the DNA is destroyed when food is processed. Surveys have found that even so, most people want the right to know if the food they are eating comes from something that has been genetically engineered, and they may have ethical reasons or concerns about environmental issues that make them want to avoid it.

- The most certain way of avoiding GE food is to eat organic produce. In the spring of 1998, the US Department of Agriculture put forward legislation which would have compromised this: they proposed that GE food could be labelled as 'organic'. Eventually these plans were rejected when they received over 280,000 letters of complaint.

- There is evidence that the United States government has been applying pressure on other countries to reject labelling regulations. A New Zealand cabinet document from 19 February 1998 showed that the US had threatened to pull out of a potential free-trade agreement with the New Zealand government because of its plans to test and label GE food. The document stated that 'The United States have told us that such an approach could impact negatively on the bilateral trade relationship and potentially end any chance of a New Zealand – United States Free Trade Agreement.'

Who is in control?

The genetic engineering industry is dominated by a handful of multi-national corporations holding interests in food, additives, pharma-

ceuticals, chemicals and seeds. These corporations are beginning to hold monopolies in the global market for genetically engineered products. This is being facilitated through:

1. The World Trade Organisation – which gives priority to free trade and makes it difficult for countries to refuse a new product or technology even if they have concerns about its potential impact on health or the environment.

2. Patenting rights – which allow corporations to patent new genetically engineered varieties. This gives them control over huge areas of the market. It is very expensive to research, develop and patent new crops, and this reinforces the trend towards market dominance by the larger companies.

3. A systematic process of acquisitions and mergers – these mergers incorporate seed companies, genetic engineering companies and other related interests. Monsanto, for example, has spent $8 billion on new acquisitions in the past three years.

'This is not just a consolidation of seed companies, it's really a consolidation of the entire food chain'

(Robert T. Fraley, co-president of Monsanto's agricultural sector)

Years of intense lobbying by the industry are beginning to pay off. Their share of a global food market now worth $2000 billion a year is increasing rapidly. Some analysts suggest that if current trends con-

tinue, the majority of the food we eat could be genetically engineered within a decade. Most of the industrialised nations have now adopted the biotech agenda as their own and are encouraging investment in genetic engineering as a route to profit and competitive advantage. Close relationships between industry and national governments are increasingly becoming causes for concern.

The United States government in particular has been criticised for 'revolving doors' between the White House and the genetic engineering industry. Many of the people now sitting on key regulatory bodies such as the Food and Drug Administration have strong links to these multi-national corporations.

In a document leaked to Greenpeace, PR firm Burson Marsteller demonstrated confidence in the proactive stance of national governments. They advised EuropaBio (a consortium of GE companies with interests in Europe) to refrain from partaking in any public debate and leave it to 'those charged with public trust, politicians and regulators, to assure the public that biotech products are safe.'

- Text written by Luke Anderson, author of *Genetic engineering, food and our environment*, Green Books, Totnes 1999.

© Greenpeace

Junk journalism unfairly taints biotech food

By Michael Fumento

On a recent visit to France, I saw a magazine cover depicting a tomato with a burning fuse and 'La Cuisine du Diable' spelled out in big bold letters below. It wasn't about a recipe for devil's-food cake with tomatoes, but about food developed through biotechnology.

A more influential magazine contains an article that could be called 'La Cuisine du Diable Lite'. September's issue of *Consumer Reports* presents a more honest look at biotechnology than the French magazine. Considering the magazine's growing tendency to find corporate-produced horrors behind every bush, that's an achievement.

Indeed, the article stated, 'There is no evidence that genetically engineered foods on the market are not safe to eat,' adding that genetic engineering could lead to consumer benefits like lower cholesterol and increased cancer resistance.

But like Darth Vader, *Consumer Reports* embraces the dark side. It repeats false claims about biotech foods, says biotech development doesn't have enough safeguards and recommends mandatory labelling of foods containing genetically engineered ingredients.

You can be sure that *Consumer Reports* wasn't about to weaken its case by explaining that there is no inherent difference between bioengineered food and nonbioengineered food. Virtually nothing we eat is truly 'natural'. From cattle to corn, apples to artichokes, today's food is the result of crossbreeding experiments dating to the dawn of history. Many plant varieties we consume didn't exist a century ago. With biotechnology, you isolate a specific gene or genes with the desired features and splice them into the organism you want to improve. It's faster, surer and safer than the old technique of crossbreeding.

Henry Miller, a senior research fellow at the Hoover Institution, notes that the few harmful plants developed before gene-splicing would have been much less likely to occur under biotechnology.

Can biotechnology guarantee food that is utterly, absolutely, 101 per cent safe? No. There is no technology that can. But biotech food regulations are at least as tough as those for other foods and often needlessly tougher.

Since biotech is merely an extension of the sort of food development that's always been going on, there's no justification for additional scrutiny.

But even major US government agencies are split — the Food and Drug Agency sees no reason for more scrutiny, while the heavily politicised Environmental Protection Agency burdens it with worthless tests. But the greatest problem for companies investing billions of dollars in these foods is not with government regulators. Rather, they suffer under a constant barrage of false claims from environmental activists, organic farmers and media crusaders. They are besieged by European governments that perceive (correctly) that their heavily subsidised farmers will need even more subsidies to compete with cheaper biotech crops.

If companies actually committed the sins they're accused of, the resulting media attention and lawsuits could destroy them. Friends of the Earth has already sent chilling notices to individual researchers warning they will personally be held legally liable for problems.

So the food is safe. Why label it then? Simple, says *Consumer Reports*: 'Consumers have a fundamental right to know what they eat.'

That sounds nice but doesn't mean much. *Consumer Reports* and other biotech labelling advocates note many European governments mandate biotech food labelling. Yet few mandate nutrition labels on food to the extent required in North America.

If we are to label biotech foods, why don't we require labels informing us where the ingredients were grown, slaughtered or synthesised? Why not tell us the specific variety of blueberry in that muffin, or grapes in that juice? Because it's not important. Since biotech food differs from other food only in the way it was developed, there's no purpose to labelling it. But activists and media allies continue to fight for such labels, in hopes that a biotech label will scare consumers away.

Furthermore, because labelling requires food testing at every stage of transport from picking to processing, it increases the cost of those foods by as much as 30 per cent.

What the public needs is a label on all the scientifically inaccurate articles and press releases on biotech food. Perhaps: 'The following piece contains five per cent half-truths, 10 per cent obfuscation and 85 per cent rubbish.'

© 1999 The London Free Press

ADDITIONAL RESOURCES

You might like to contact the following organisations for further information. Due to the increasing cost of postage, many organisations cannot respond to enquiries unless they receive a stamped, addressed envelope.

Consumers' Association
2 Marylebone Road
London, NW1 4DF
Tel: 0171 830 6000
Fax: 0171 830 7600
E-mail: which@which.co.uk
Web site: www.which.net
A research and policy organisation providing a vigorous and independent voice for domestic consumers in the UK.

Department of the Environment, Transport and the Regions (DETR)
Eland House
Bressenden Place
London, SW1E 5DU
Tel: 0171 890 3000
Fax: 0171 890 5229
Web site: www.detr.gov.uk
Publishes booklets and extracts from relevant reports on transport-related issues.

European Food Information Council (EUFIC)
1 Place des Pyramides 75001
Paris, France
Tel: 00 33 140 20 44 40
Fax: 00 33 140 20 44 41
E-mail: eufic@eufic.org
Web site: www.eufic.org
EUFIC is a non-profit-making organisation based in Paris. It has been established to provide science-based information on foods and food-related topics i.e. nutrition and health, food safety and quality and biotechnology in food for the attention of European consumers. It publishes regular newsletters, leaflets, reviews, case studies and other background information on food issues.

Food and Drink Federation
6 Catherine Street
London, WC2B 5JJ
Tel: 0171 836 2460
Fax: 0171 836 0580
Web site: www.foodfuture.org.uk
Produces publications and surveys on food and biotechnology.

Friends of the Earth
26-28 Underwood Street
London, N1 7JQ
Tel: 0171 490 1555
Fax: 0171 490 0881
E-mail: info@foe.co.uk
Web site: www.foe.co.uk
As an independent environmental group, Friends of the Earth publishes a comprehensive range of leaflets, books and in-depth briefings and reports.

Greenpeace
Canonbury Villas
London, N1 2PN
Tel: 0171 865 8100
Fax: 0171 865 8200
E-mail: gn-info@uk.greenpeace.org
Web site: www.greenpeace.org.uk
Protects the environment through peaceful direct action. Actions on land and sea against whaling, nuclear power, air and water pollution and the exploitation of wildlife.

Monsanto Plc
47 Albemarle Street
London, W1X 3FE
Tel: 0171 495 8455
Fax: 0171 495 8361
Web site: www.monsanto.co.uk
As a life sciences company, Monsanto is committed to finding solutions to the growing global needs for food and health by sharing common forms of science and technology among agriculture, nutrition and health.
Our family of 30,000 employees worldwide seeks to make and market high-value agricultural products, pharmaceuticals and food ingredients in a manner that achieves environmental sustainability.

Society, Religion and Technology Project (SRTP)
John Knox House
45 High Street
Edinburgh, EH1 1SR
Tel: 0131 556 2953
Fax: 0131 556 7478
E-mail: srtp@srtp.org.uk
Web site: www.srtp.org.uk
SRTP is a project of the Church of Scotland set up in 1970 to examine ethical issues emerging from modern technology and to engage with key scientists and policy makers. It seeks to provide balanced and informed insights on major current issues. Its work includes genetic engineering, cloning, patenting, risk, environment, energy and 'God and Science' issues. It produces information sheets on a wide variety of issues which are available from the above address. Also has produced a book called *Engineering Genesis* published by Earthscan, edited by Donald Bruce and Ann Bruce, published November 1998, reprinted with updates November 1999, price £14.50.

The Soil Association
Bristol House
40-56 Victoria Street
Bristol, BS1 6BY
Tel: 0117 929 0661
Fax: 0117 925 2504
E-mail: info@soilassociation.org
Web site: www.soilassociation.org
Works to educate the general public about organic agriculture, gardening and food, and their benefits for both human health and the environment.

INDEX

The Internet has been likened to shopping in a supermarket without aisles. The press of a button on a Web browser can bring up thousands of sites but working your way through them to find what you want can involve long and frustrating on-line searches. And unfortunately many sites contain inaccurate, misleading or heavily biased information. Our researchers have therefore undertaken an extensive analysis to bring you a selection of quality Web site addresses.

* * * * *

BioIndustry Association
www.bioindustry.org
The BioIndustry Association exists to encourage and promote a financially sound and thriving sector of the UK economy built on developments across the biosciences to create wealth, employment and an expanding skills base. Useful articles on GM food here.

The Soil Association
www.soilassociation.org
Click on the Library button, then go to Briefing Papers. Here you will find a range of articles which outline the views of the Soil Association on GM issues. The GMO link is also worth a look.

Food and Drink Federation
www.foodfuture.org.uk
This site aims to inform consumers about both sides of the GM debate. It provides a clear and comprehensible explanation of the benefits which biotechnology could bring to our food supply. Importantly, it also recognises that many people have concerns about the new technology. Well worth visiting.

The Campaign for Food Safety
www.purefood.org
Deals with issues of food safety and genetic engineering and tries to promote the growth of organic and sustainable agriculture practices – both in the US and globally. Provides information, interviews, and background material for journalists, news organisations, and public interest activists world-wide.

Friends of the Earth
www.foe.co.uk
Lots of information here on GM foods with links on such issues as: the Real Food Campaign, the problems, what you can do, GM in depth, Who's in control?, and a shoppers' guide.

Greenpeace
www.greenpeace.org.uk
Click on the search button and enter GM food. This will bring up a range of interesting articles.

Society, Religion and Technology Project
www.srtp.org.uk
This site aims to bring professional expertise and provide informed and penetrating comment for technologists, educators, media, the Church, the public – in fact anyone with an interest in how technology is affecting our lives, and the issues it raises. For their views on GM food, scroll down the home page to Genetically Modified Food – Precaution but not a Moratorium. This leads to a wide range of articles about GM issues.

Monsanto plc
www.monsanto.co.uk
Monsanto's web site is about food biotechnology in the UK and around the world. It explains the potential for genetically modified food to contribute to a better environment and a sustainable, plentiful, and healthy food supply. They recognise, however, that many consumers have genuine concerns about food biotechnology and its impact on their families.

ACKNOWLEDGEMENTS

The publisher is grateful for permission to reproduce the following material.

While every care has been taken to trace and acknowledge copyright, the publisher tenders its apology for any accidental infringement or where copyright has proved untraceable. The publisher would be pleased to come to a suitable arrangement in any such case with the rightful owner.

Chapter One: An Overview

Biotechnology basics, © European Food Information Council (EUFIC), *The benefits*, © Food and Drink Federation, *Genetic modification of major crops*, © Food and Drink Federation, *The concerns*, © Food and Drink Federation, *Where GM foods are grown*, © Telegraph Group Limited, London 1999.

Chapter Two: The GM Debate

Questions about genetically modified organisms, © St. James's Palace and the Press Association Ltd 1999, *Ten comments from a puzzled subject*, © Food and Drink Federation, *GM foods*, © The Guardian, June 1999, *Genetically modified food*, © Donald M. Bruce, 1998, *Concern over GM crops*, © MORI/ Greenpeace, *Biotech primer*, © Monsanto, *Genewatch*, © MORI/Genewatch, *Public attitudes towards genetic engineering*, © MORI, *Doctors call for GM food ban to ease public fears*, © Telegraph Group Limited, London 1999, *Genetic science hailed by Blair*, © Telegraph Group Limited, London 1999, *What's wrong with genetic engineering*, © Friends of the Earth, GM *food 'no worse than traditional plant crops'*, © Telegraph Group Limited, London 1999, *Genetic engineering and human health*, © The Soil Association, *A question of breeding*, © New Scientist, RBI limited 1999, *Genetic engineering*, © The Soil Association, GM *crops 'can fight Third World hunger'*, © Telegraph Group Limited, London 1999, *Regulation of GM crops*, © Food and Drink Federation, October 1999, *What about . . . a moratorium*, © Food and Drink Federation, *Gone with the wind*, © New Scientist, RBI limited 1999, *Test of the revolution*, © The Guardian, August 1999, *Genetically modified organisms*, © English Nature Press Office, June 1999, *Food for the future*, © The Guardian, August 1999, *Protecting the consumer interest*, © Which On-line, *Genetic engineering and consumer choice*, © The Soil Association, *If we fear technology, we really fear ourselves*, © 1999 The Irish Times, *Genetically engineered food*, © Greenpeace, *Junk journalism unfairly taints biotech food*, © 1999 The London Free Press.

Photographs and illustrations:

Pages 1, 10, 15, 21, 29, 33, 34, 37: Pumpkin House, pages 9, 12, 18, 19, 27, 30, 32, 35, 39: Simon Kneebone.

Craig Donnellan
Cambridge
January, 2000